JOHN

The Beloved Gospel

Jon Paulien

Pacific Press® Publishing Association
Nampa, Idaho
Oshawa, Ontario, Canada
www.pacificpress.com

Designed by Dennis Ferree
Cover illustration by Justinen Creative Group

Unless otherwise noted, all Scripture quotations are from the
New International Version.

Additional copies of this book are available through the following:
Phone: 1-800-765-6955
Internet: www.adventistbookcenter.com

Library of Congress Cataloging-in-Publication Data

Paulien, Jon, 1949-
John : the beloved Gospel / Jon Paulien.
p. cm.
ISBN: 0-8163-2000-4
1. Bible. N.T. John—Devotional literature. I. Title.

BS2615.54.P38 2003
226.5'06—dc21   2003054943

03 04 05 06 07 • 5 4 3 2 1

Dedication

This book is dedicated to Ed Dickerson,
my best friend and favorite Sabbath School teacher.
He has always inspired me to be the best person
and teacher I can be.

Table of Contents

Chapter 1   The Unique Purpose of John's Gospel 7

Chapter 2   Jesus Is the Best 16

Chapter 3   Something Better 24

Chapter 4   Grace Is All-Inclusive 32

Chapter 5   The Struggle to Be Real 42

Chapter 6   Putting the Past Behind You 51

Chapter 7   The Sacred in the Common 60

Chapter 8   At the Feast of Tabernacles 68

Chapter 9   A Devoted Soul and an Impending Cross 78

Chapter 10   Real Greatness 89

Chapter 11   The Spirit Replaces Jesus 99

Chapter 12   Jesus Lays Down His Life for His Friends 109

Chapter 13   The Power of the Resurrection 118

CHAPTER 1

The Unique Purpose of John's Gospel

"Wow, is she ever beautiful!" "What a personality!" "The man of my dreams!" "It doesn't get any better than this!" "I've never been so happy in my life!"

I first experienced romantic love when I was a teenager back in the big city. Though I had no illusions that the girl I fell for was the most beautiful girl in the world, she sure looked beautiful to me! Not knowing how she felt about me at first, I consulted with people who knew her to find out where she lived and how she traveled to school. Then I went out of my way to hang around certain subway platforms just to catch a glimpse of her as she went by.

I found excuses to attend her church instead of my own. I watched for her in the halls between classes. Long before I saw her I could sense when she had entered a crowded room. When I learned that she cared as much about me as I did about her, finding time with her became the highest priority of my school day.

The best block of time was the commute home. I lived an hour and a half away in another state (first subway, then bus). But I would ride the subway all the way to her station first, even though it was quite a bit out of my way. Sometimes we would buy time for conversation by letting three, four, or even six or seven trains pass before boarding one on the way to her place. Everything else took second place to finding time to spend together.

Relationship is all about being together, spending time with each other, talking and listening, doing things together. When you love someone, you want to spend time with that person.

According to the Gospel of John, the most important relationship you will ever have is the one you form with Jesus. John wrote his Gospel to help us fall in love with Jesus and to show us how to spend time with Him even though we can't see, hear, or touch Him directly.

John wrote that the key to eternal life is to know God (17:3). Jesus came down to this earth not only to show us what God is like, but also to offer us a relationship with God (15:1-8). To know Jesus is to know God (14:9). To know Jesus is to have eternal life.

For the Gospel of John, then, the key to Christian experience is to get to know Jesus personally—to become His friend, to live with Him, talk to Him, experience Him. When we do this, we are brought into intimate relationship with God. We can be as close to God as branches are to the vine that nourishes and supports them.

But how do we do that in a secular world? *How do we have a relationship with someone we can't see or hear or touch?* How do we know Jesus when the fleeting images of television and the Internet seem more real than God?

As Good as His Touch

Have you ever felt that those who knew Jesus in the flesh had an advantage over us? Have you ever felt that it would be easier to be a Christian if Jesus lived next door and you could talk to Him face to face? The generation to whom the Gospel of John was written felt the same way.

It seems that the Fourth Gospel was written when its author, the "beloved disciple," was nearing death. He was the last living link with the first generation of Christians—those who had known Jesus in the flesh (see 21:20-23). John's approaching death threatened to plunge the second generation of Christians into confusion and uncertainty. What would become of them without the guidance of those who had known and talked to Jesus in person?

The Gospel's statement of purpose (20:30, 31) follows the "doubting Thomas" story (20:24-29). Jesus told Thomas, "Because you have seen me, you have believed; blessed are those who have not seen and yet have believed" (v. 29). Comparing that verse with the statement that follows in the next verse makes it clear that Thomas represents all the disciples who had seen and touched Jesus—the first generation of Jesus' followers. The second generation of Christians followed Jesus without that privilege. Jesus' blessing in verse 29 was not for Thomas and the other first-generation disciples; it was for the second generation, those who had come to faith apart from physical contact with Jesus.

That brings us to the question that led us into this study: How do we develop a relationship with Jesus when we can't see Him, hear Him, or touch Him? The Gospel of John was carefully designed to answer that question. Its answer becomes clear when we compare its portrayal of Jesus' miracles with those of Matthew, Mark, and Luke. Each of these other Gospels pictures Jesus repeatedly using touch in the performance of His miracles (see, for example, Matt. 8:3, 4, 14, 15; 9:18-25; Mark 1:29-31, 40-42; 5:21-43; Luke 4:40; 5:12, 13; 7:14, 15). But such touching is remarkably absent in the Gospel of John.

At the wedding of Cana (2:1-11) the water turns into wine without any physical contact on Jesus' part. Jesus heals the royal official's son in Capernaum while remaining in Cana, some sixteen miles away (4:46-54). Jesus heals the paralytic at the pool of Bethesda without touching him (5:1-15). He *does* smear a little clay into a blind man's eyes, but the healing doesn't happen until the man washes his eyes in the Pool of Siloam, more than half a mile away (9:6, 7). Jesus *calls* Lazarus from the tomb—He doesn't shake him or drag him out (11:41-43).

The common denominator of all these "signs" is the lack of physical contact between Jesus and the objects of His miraculous attention. Why is this important? It showed that distance was no barrier to the reception of Jesus' blessings. So, the second generation's lack of personal contact with Jesus placed them at no disadvantage.

Note also that it was the words of Jesus that accomplished each of these miracles. To the servants at the wedding of Cana He said, "Fill and draw" (2:7, 8). To the royal official He said, "Go, your son lives" (4:50). To the paralytic He said, "Rise, take up your bed and walk" (5:8, NKJ). To the blind man He said, "Go, wash" (9:7). To Lazarus He said, "Come out" (11:43). In each case it was the words of Jesus, not His physical touch, that accomplished His intention.

These scenes taught the second generation of Christians the power of Jesus' words to overcome barriers of space. *His word is as good as His touch!* His word is as powerful at a distance as it is close at hand. It is through that Word that the Holy Spirit ministers to the needs of the second generation (14:26, 27).

We today share in the second generation's deficiency. We, too, would love to have the privilege of Thomas, whose faith was fully confirmed by sight. We, too, would appreciate a face-to-face relationship with Jesus. But the Gospel of John tells us that the seeming absence of God in our time raises no barrier to the mighty working of Jesus through the Spirit. *His Word is as good as His touch.* Though ministered through a mere printed page, it still retains its power to save and to heal. All the benefits that were available through the physical presence of Jesus are now available through His Word!

John's Gospel also teaches us how to gain these benefits. In each of its miracle stories, some human party had to carry out the words of Jesus in order for the miracle to take place. The servants had to pour water before they could draw wine. The paralytic had to rise and gather his bedding. The blind man had to go to the Pool of Siloam and wash.

So, John's Gospel tells us two things: First, we must know the words of Jesus and discern their application to our particular situation. Careful study of the Gospel of John becomes the great, living replacement for the face-to-face relationship that the disciples had with Jesus. And second, we must carry out what Jesus commands. We experience the power of Jesus through the Spirit only when we obey His words.

The Fourth Gospel was written so that those who had not seen might believe (20:29-31). As we read and apply the Gospel, we obtain the life that Jesus shared when He was physically on this earth.

Building the Relationship

Relationships between people are grounded on three things: talking, listening, and doing things together. The same basic dynamics are crucial to a relationship with Jesus. If we wish to have a relationship with Jesus, we need to spend time talking with Him, listening to Him, and doing things with Him. Let me summarize some of the key principles of a devotional relationship with Jesus.

1. Talking to Jesus

The basic means of talking to Jesus is prayer. Yet many Christians of all ages have struggled to make prayer work for them. How can you and I do better?

(1) Be flexible. Don't be locked in to any particular position for prayer. In other words, the primary thing is not your physical position: whether you're on your knees or your eyes are open or shut. A careful look at the prayers described in the Bible indicates that there is no one right position for prayer. The right position for you is the one that best helps you connect with God.

(2) Try writing out some of your prayers. It is amazing what the process of writing does to help concentrate your mind on the reality of being in the act of prayer. Computer wizards may find a notebook computer the most effective way to do this.

(3) Be relevant. When you pray, focus on the things that truly matter to you. Prayer tends to become repetitive and ritualistic when it is focused on things that are not of ultimate concern to you. Talk to God about the things in your life that matter the most to you.

(4) Thank God in very specific ways. Thank Him for air, water, the color of the carpet, the bird you just saw out the window. This may seem a bit silly at first, but where would you be without air? What would life be like without color, without animals and birds? The best way to find the joy of the Lord (Neh. 8:10) is through a spirit of gratitude and praise. The best way to develop such an attitude is to learn to thank God for everything you receive.

2. Listening to Jesus

How do you listen to Someone whose voice you cannot hear? The primary method, of course, is to hear Jesus' voice in Scripture. As we've noted, a major theme of this book of John's is that Jesus' words in the written Gospel are as powerful and effective as His spoken words and physical touch were to those who knew Him in the flesh.

How can you study Scripture in such a way as to bring you into a living relationship with Jesus?

(1) Choose relevant readings. To be devotionally useful, Scripture reading must be relevant to present experience, to things that matter in practical terms. Genealogies and prophecies may be of intense intellectual interest, but they may not offer practical guidance for the daily issues of the household, the workplace, and the neighborhood.

(2) Focus on Jesus. Since a personal knowledge of Jesus Christ is the most relevant of all spiritual concerns, devotional study needs to focus on Jesus. The Gospel of John is far more relevant to this purpose than 1 Chronicles or Judges, for example.

(3) Take your time. When you're reading devotionally, focus on discerning God's voice to you personally, not on covering a certain number of pages or mastering a certain amount of information. Allow the reading to sink in—let it impact the very core of your being!

(4) Write out special insights. Write down or enter into your computer the "highlight-film" kind of insights that God gives you as part of your devotional experience. We tend to forget what we don't write down. You'll never find another devotional book as effective for you as the one you write for yourself. The insights you write down can help you rekindle your walk with Jesus in tough times.

(5) Keep a spiritual diary of your experiences, dialogues, and struggles with God. Don't limit yourself to devotional note taking—challenge your experience with God. Ask Him direct questions such as, "How do You feel about the way I relate to my family? Am I being sensitive to Your leading in my life right now? Is there someone in my life who needs to hear about You right now?"

(6) Let God answer your prayers. When you have finished praying, stay on your knees. Keep a pad of paper in front of you, and when your prayer is through, pick up your pencil and wait. You've talked to God about the things that matter most to you, and you're now in a position to receive. So, write down whatever comes to mind. Don't try to evaluate what you've written; treat this as spiritual brainstorming.

3. Working together with Jesus

Without concrete and practical faith-action, however, the study and prayer life can easily become confined to a closet separate from the rest of our experience. What happens in our devotional life will have little impact on our everyday experience if we don't consciously combine it with corresponding action.

(1) Sharing faith is not optional. Expression deepens impression. If you talk faith, you will have more faith. Sharing your faith with others strengthens and confirms your own faith.

(2) Stretch the limits. Don't be afraid to do something radical with God. Do a short-term mission project in a part of the world much different from yours. (It doesn't have to be overseas.) Plant a garden, dedicate a portion as a special gift to God, and see what happens. Shared risk enhances intimacy with others. Risking yourself for God enhances intimacy with God.

(3) Walk the talk. How you live has a powerful impact on what you believe. This is why evangelists call people to come forward to

express their commitment. There is something about getting out of one's seat and walking to the front that nails down a decision in a way that very few other things can do. Action has a powerful impact on belief and experience.

(4) Act on impressions. After the spiritual brainstorming mentioned in the previous section, experiment with the ideas that came to your mind. Some may be from God and others merely from the fog of your own dreams or confusion. As you experiment with these impressions, you will gradually learn to discern which impressions come from God and which do not.

John wrote his Gospel to provide life for a new generation of Christians—those who didn't have face-to-face contact with Jesus. That life becomes real as we apply the words of Jesus to the problems of life.

CHAPTER 2

Jesus Is the Best

John 1:1-18

Have you ever seen a cricket or some other bug in church? Have you ever wondered what its life was like—how it viewed the world? As far as the cricket in church is concerned, his entire universe is an auditorium. Can you see him taking his daughter out at night and telling her to look up at the ceiling? He strokes her back shell with one of his clickers and sighs, "It's a mighty big sky we live under, girl." Does he know that he sees only a fraction of the world?

Crickets also have rather limited hopes and dreams. A cricket's highest dream is to find a piece of bread. He falls asleep amid visions of pie crumbs and jam drippings. And consider the hero of the cricket's world. Crickets cheer for the most talented members of their species. The speedster who dashes across a room full of feet without being squashed. The gutsy one who has explored the hinterland of the baptistry. The courageous one who has ventured to the edge of a mighty cabinet or hopped along the precipice of a windowsill.

Whom do you suppose a cricket worships? Does she acknowledge that there was a creative hand behind the construction of the church she lives in? Or does she choose to worship the building itself or perhaps a particular place within the building? Does she assume that since she has never seen the builder, there was no builder?

Perhaps some crickets become intellectually advanced and engage in philosophical questions such as, "Is there life beyond the auditorium?" Some crickets believe some living being must have created the place. How else would the lights come on? How else could air blow through the vents? How else could music fill the room? Out of amazement for what they can see, they worship what they can't see and can't explain.

Other crickets disagree. They explain that the lights come on because of electricity, the air blows because of air conditioners, and music is the result of stereos and speakers. "There is no life beyond this room," they declare. "All we have to do is figure out how everything works."

Like crickets, none of us human beings does well at imagining life beyond the limits of what we can see and experience. Because we've never seen the hand that made the universe, we may assume that there is no life beyond the here and now. We may assume that there is no purpose beyond our own pleasure, that there is nothing eternal and no divine factor in existence. Like a cricket that refuses to acknowledge a builder, we may refuse to acknowledge our Creator.

In light of this, John 1 tells an amazing story. It is as if the builder of the church became a cricket and entered the church to help the crickets understand a far greater reality than they could possibly grasp on the basis of their limited vision. In the prologue to John, we catch a glimpse beyond our limited "room" and touch base with the Creator Himself! Wonder of wonders, the Creator Himself came down and walked among us, learned our language, and showed us in human terms what God is like.

Walking Through the Prologue

The first part of the prologue to the Gospel of John (1:1-5) focuses on the nature and pre-existence of the One who came down from heaven to dwell with the human race. In the Greek language, the language in which John originally wrote his Gospel, the message of this passage is abundantly clear. Before Creation, the Word was already in existence. He was fully God, yet a Person distinct from the Father. He was the God of Creation. Not a single thing was made apart from Him.

This opening passage prepares us to realize that the One who walked this earth, who became sweaty, tired, and hungry, was intimate with God before the world began. Although He became part of the human race and was subject to human limitations, He was the One who created the human race and the world in which we live.

The middle part of the prologue (1:9-13) tells us that the divine, creative Word came down from heaven and entered this world. Most of the human race reject Him, but those who believe in Him become children of God! The supernatural, creative power of the Word produces a new birth, totally apart from human effort or planning. So, becoming a child of God is as much a miracle as the original act of Creation (cp. 1:1-3). From beginning to end, Christian life is a gift from God.

The prologue moves to a stirring conclusion in verses 14-18. Though the Word always "was" (see verse 1), verse 14 says He "became"—in the original Greek, the same term used in John 1:3 and Genesis 1 to describe the original Creation. The Word went from being "with God" to being "with us" (vs. 1, 2; cp. v. 14). Though he "was God" (v. 1), He "became flesh" (v. 14). With this shift of language, John shows that the Word is both divine and human; Jesus Christ must be both to save us.

John 1:14-18 compares Jesus to the Old Testament sanctuary, to John the Baptist, and to Moses. "Made his dwelling" (v. 14) translates the Greek word for "pitch his tent," a reminder of the tabernacle in the wilderness (Exod. 25:8-9). The glory of Jesus that the disciples saw recalls the glory of the Shekinah in that tabernacle (Exod. 40:34, 35). This allusion to the Old Testament sanctuary explains the "grace in place of grace" of John 1:16. The Old Testament sanctuary was a marvelous source of grace and blessing. But Jesus is a better revelation of God than even the sanctuary was, because in Jesus, God dwelt directly in human flesh, and we could behold what before had been hidden behind curtains.

Jesus' superiority is also proclaimed in verse 15 of the prologue. There John the Baptist compares Jesus to himself. He says, "He who comes after me has surpassed me because he was before me." Jesus' greatness is not based on *when* He came, but on *who He was before He came.*

Verses 17 and 18 compare Jesus with Moses. Jesus offers a better revelation of God than even Moses did, though he made the ultimate revelation of God in the Old Testament. While the "law" was given by Moses, grace and truth came into being ("were created"—the same Greek word as in verses 3 and 14) through Jesus Christ. John then asserts, "No one has ever seen God." In actual fact, Moses did see God, but only His back (Exod. 33:18-23; 34:4-7). In contrast to Moses, however, Jesus is "at the Father's side," or more accurately, "face to face" with Him. The One who was always "with God" (John 1:1, 2), who is now again at the Father's side (1:18)—this is the One who was made flesh and dwelt among us (1:14). What a revelation! Jesus is the best!

So, the prologue to John interprets everything that happens in the Gospel in the larger perspective of eternity. Many of the Jews of the first century regarded John the Baptist and Moses as the two greatest human personages. They revered John as a contemporary prophet and Moses as the great deliverer of Israel and giver of the Law. But Jesus was even greater than the greatest men known to the people of the time. He was the best because He was God made flesh. He enabled human beings to know what God is really like.

What Would Jesus Do?

In the prologue to the Gospel of John we get a glimpse of what Jesus was like from eternity. We also get a glimpse of His humanity and His rejection by "His own." But there is one aspect of Jesus' life that this Gospel does not address: His birth and childhood. And while Matthew and Luke mention His birth, only Luke gives us any glimpse at all of Jesus' childhood (Luke 2:40-51). Luke 2:52 tells us: "Jesus kept increasing in wisdom and stature, and in favor with God and men"(NAS). We learn from this statement that He matured physically, mentally, and spiritually through His teen years and into young adulthood and that most people appreciated Him.

The Gospels mainly picture His three-and-a-half-year ministry, concluding with His death, burial, and ascension. In other words, the example Jesus left us in the Gospels concerns how one should behave in the course of active ministry. It's not surprising, then, that many new Christians try immediately to get into formal church ministry, regardless of their skills, gifts, or temperament. It seems far easier to apply the example of Jesus to ministry than to everyday life.

But "what would Jesus do" in the course of ordinary, everyday life? How did Jesus live and deal with people when He was building homes and furniture instead of preaching, teaching, and healing? How did Jesus behave at synagogue potlucks? What was Jesus like as a teenager when He was playing with the other kids? What difference did He make in His neighborhood? I often wish the Gospel writers had included more information about this period of Jesus' life. The carpenters, bus drivers, cooks, factory and office workers, scientists, and janitors of this world would appreciate knowing how Jesus handled the stresses of humdrum existence. But the biblical evidence is minimal, as we have seen.

However, in a chapter entitled "Days of Conflict" in the book *The Desire of Ages,* Ellen White amplified the meager picture of Luke 2. Her description of Jesus as a teen is most interesting. Here we catch a glimpse of how Jesus would respond to people if He were placed in ordinary circumstances in today's world. I have distilled Ellen White's account into five guiding principles that seem to have ruled Jesus' life before His ministry began.

1. He maintained an independent spirit based on principle. As a youth, rather than merely following rules made by others, Jesus grounded His religious experience on principles. He did not attack the practices of the leaders in the church, He just submitted His everyday decisions to the principles of the Scriptures. When the leaders reproved Him for not obeying a rule, He always pointed them to the Bible as the justification for His conduct. So, young Christians should not be forced into predetermined molds. They should be allowed to experience the creativity of the Spirit in their application of Scripture to everyday life.

2. He tried to please others. Jesus' independence was not the independence of a contentious rebel. He was not different just to be different. He diverged from custom only when obedience to

God's Word required it. In a gentle and submissive way He tried to please everyone He met. He was tactful. He was always sympathetic to those who suffered; He helped them carry their burdens, both physical and psychological. He treated everyone with kindness. And He did all He could to be at peace with all He met.

3. He met opposition head-on. Jesus' gentleness and tact, however, did not mean that He was a doormat who could be swayed by intimidation. While kind toward those who disagreed with Him, He remained faithful to biblical principle. His firmness often got Him in trouble with the religious leaders and even with His family. He suffered particularly at the hands of His older brothers, who accused Him of stubbornness and disregard for the faith of their fathers. They charged Him with thinking Himself superior to them and to the religious teachers. They tried to intimidate Him. They were jealous, yet contemptuous.

Jesus' mother, pressured by His brothers and the religious leaders, would also get in His face and urge Him to conform to the practices of the time. She loved Him dearly, but was frustrated by His refusal to conform. The discord both in and outside the home complicated her life, but Jesus' Scripture-based principles did not allow any easy fixes. We should not expect that following Jesus will lead to a placid and comfortable life.

4. He was inclusive. Jesus particularly disregarded traditions that involved exclusiveness. He was open to relationship with all people, regardless of their religion or lifestyle. He helped whoever needed help and was cheerful about it. He would often skip meals to feed people who were needier than He. In His glorious lack of prejudice toward people of all heritages and backgrounds, He was a living demonstration of the gospel.

Because He challenged the walls of religious exclusiveness, He was often more at home at the margins of society than in the mainstream. The people at the margins enjoyed His presence because He was always cheerful, kind, helpful, and interesting. He taught outcasts that they were endowed by God with precious talents, which they could use to make a mighty difference in the world. He treated no human being as worthless.

Yet even at the margins of society, His life was not easy. While Jesus was never impatient in word or look, He could not witness sin or abuse without pain that was impossible to disguise. People accused Him of being too narrow and straitlaced. Jesus was too independent for the religious people and too straitlaced for the irreligious! And because His life condemned their evil, many retaliated by casting contempt on Him regarding His birth.

5. He found strength in God. To cope with these difficulties, Jesus spent significant amounts of time away from people, out in nature. There He would search the Scriptures and talk with God. Afterward, He would come back refreshed and ready to face whatever life held for that day. If Jesus needed that kind of relationship with God in order to cope, think how much more we need it!

Why should we pay special attention to the life of Jesus? Because the prologue to John's Gospel teaches us that a Child in first-century Galilee was greater than the sanctuary, greater than Moses, greater than John the Baptist. He was the living representation in human flesh of the character of God. In Jesus we are lifted beyond the limitations of human perception to gain a clear grasp of eternity. Jesus—and only Jesus—can truly teach us what God would be like if He lived among us.

CHAPTER 3

Something Better

John 1:19–2:22

Another day, another shekel. Business has been really good for a while, Micah the caterer thought to himself. *Lots of young people growing up, lots of marriages to celebrate, lots of food and drink to prepare.* People needed caterers for such occasions. It provided a decent living and a lot of satisfaction—helping families get together, seeing happy people enjoying a good feast.

This particular wedding was a bit strange, however. Mary, the wife of Joseph, had approached Micah about catering a wedding for a relative of hers.[1] It was rumored that Mary considered her son Yeshuah to be born of the Holy Spirit and that perhaps he was the long awaited Messiah. *That's a novel claim for a woman who was caught pregnant when she was young and single!* Micah thought.

Some people were concerned that Yeshuah's arrival with his disciples would create a sideshow that would detract from the wedding itself. But something even worse happened. No caterer could ever let supplies run out before a party was over. That could result in an irreparable blow to one's reputation, especially in a small town like Cana. But that was apparently about to happen. Micah began to panic as he noticed a decline in the quality of the grape juice being served. You see, the right way to cater drinks was to serve the best stuff first. Then, when people were a bit tired of feasting and could no longer tell the difference, one could bring out the inferior drink. That strategy saved lots of money, much of which went into Micah's pockets. But it also meant that when the quality declined, the quantity was starting to run low. And the party was far from over.

That's when the strangest thing happened. Just as supplies were running out, a servant brought Micah a cup of juice to try. It was the sweetest, freshest-tasting juice he had ever drunk. And there was plenty to go around! Now he *knew* these people were strange—saving the best drink for the end of the feast! That just didn't make any sense! That wasn't the way things were supposed to go—everybody knew that! Micah hoped that this wasn't going to set any precedents for the future.

One last strange thing: Micah didn't remember ordering this particular brand of juice. . . .

A Simple Story?

John 2 opens with what seems to be a simple story about a wedding where the drink runs out before the end of the feast. But Jesus shows up and rescues a young couple and their caterer from embarrassment. Is that all there is to this story, or is something deeper going on?

Surprisingly, the Gospel of John records no parables. Since parables were a major basis for Jesus' teaching in Matthew, Mark, and Luke, their absence in John is quite remarkable. In this Gospel, however, real-life stories about Jesus fill the role played by parables in the other Gospels. And beneath its surface, each historical account in John teaches something special about Jesus. John's "parables" are not hypothetical stories. They are real events that were lived by real people.

Two interesting points lie just below the surface of John 2:1-11. First, changing water into wine symbolized something bigger than a mere physical miracle. The water was not just any water. It was water set aside by the Jews for ceremonial washings (2:6). Religious people of Jesus' day often seemed obsessed with washing rituals (see Matt. 15:1, 2). Washing is good. It is sanitary. And as a religious expression, it can remind one of God. But Jesus brings something even better than ceremonial washings. He presents the tasty juice of the grape, a symbol of His blood. And this wine is not just any wine, it is "the best" (see 2:10).

Second, the story contains a series of indirect references to the Cross. The wedding took place "on the third day" (v. 1), a reference to Jesus' resurrection (see Matt. 16:21; Luke 24:7, 21, 46; Acts 10:40; 1 Cor. 15:4). Jesus turned water into wine, a symbol of His blood (Luke 22:20; 1 Cor. 11:25, 26). References to both Jesus' "time" (John 2:4, "hour" in the Greek; cp. John 7:30; 8:20; 12:23, 24) and His "glory" (John 2:11; cp. John 12:23, 24, 37-41; 17:1-5) point to the Cross. And the only two times this Gospel portrays Jesus speaking to His mother, it says He calls her "woman": in the wedding story here (2:4) and at the cross itself (19:25-27). So, in a special way, this charming wedding story becomes a parable of the Cross and of the glory of God's character that would be revealed there.

Cleansing the Temple

The story that follows—Jesus' cleansing of the temple (John 2:13-22)—also contains the two themes we have just observed:

26

Jesus replacing rituals with Himself and anticipations of the Cross. The animals being sold in the temple courts were available for sacrifices, making the "marketplace" a genuine service to long-distance travelers. The money-exchanging was necessary because the temple did business only in a unique temple currency. While other sources suggest that the temple court sales involved a lot of deception and corruption, that doesn't seem to be the issue here in John.

We get a clearer picture of the point John intended this story to make when we compare his account with those in the other three Gospels. The main similarity between all four accounts is the portrayal of Jesus driving out the people who were selling things in the temple courts. John is unique in placing the story of a temple cleansing at the beginning of Jesus' ministry instead of at the end. Also unique to John are the quotation from Psalms in verse 17, Jesus' use of a whip, the involvement of sheep and oxen, and the comments about destroying the temple and replacing it with Jesus' body.

Matthew, Mark, and Luke say that while God intended the temple to be a house of prayer, the selling has made it a "den of robbers" (Matt. 21:13; Mark 11:17; Luke 19:46). In Matthew, Jesus replaces the selling with healing (Matt. 21:13, 14). Mark, on the other hand, emphasizes that the temple is for all nations (Mark 11:17). And in Luke, Jesus simply restores the court to its original purpose: prayer and teaching (Luke 19:46, 47). But in John, something more is going on: The cleansing of the temple becomes a foretaste of Jesus' death and resurrection (John 2:19-21).

John's point is that while the activity in the temple was meeting a legitimate need, it was also distracting people from the deeper meaning of the temple services. Jesus had come to replace the sacrificial animals with His own body (John 2:21). For John, then, this story shows that the Cross is the ultimate expression of true religion. It is the ultimate revelation of God's self-sacrificing love (John 3:14; 12:32).

In John 2:1-22, therefore, we see good things (the temple and religious washings) getting in the way of the best. It is no different today. Everyone seeks meaning and a sense of value out of life, but few seek it in Jesus. Instead, people try to find "life" by accumulating things, by performing successfully, and by developing relationships with people they admire.

Good, Better, and Best

Chester thought you could find life in possessions. He grew up in the drug-infested streets of "Fort Apache"—the South Bronx section of New York City. Many of the young people in his neighborhood admired pimps and prostitutes because they drove fancy cars and wore fancy clothes. When I asked Chester what he thought happiness was, he said, "Happiness is a big, black Cadillac!" He believed that the quantity of things one possessed and could show off determined one's quality of life.

I'm more susceptible to the performance trap. If I perform well and others praise me for it, I feel more valuable as a person. This came home to me the day I made four errors at third base in a softball game. I was depressed for three days afterward. How stupid! Yet how real! Many people would give almost anything to be a sports hero or a movie star—to be considered the best in the world at what they do.

Other people evaluate life in terms of "who you know." If they have a close relationship with someone among the richest, the brightest, the most famous, or the most powerful people in their world, they feel more valuable as a human being. Often, people commit adultery, not because someone is prettier or nicer than their spouse, but because they want to be affirmed and held valuable by someone they esteem more than their spouse.

Possessions, performance, and people are good things, but they are not the best things. If true life were found in possessions, performance, and people, NBA basketball players would be the happiest people on earth. They make millions of dollars a year, they perform at the highest possible level, and they have all the romantic options anyone could possibly want. Why then is drug abuse a major issue in professional basketball? Why are some players so angry and dysfunctional? Because life—real life—cannot be found in possessions, performance, and people alone.

No matter how many possessions you have, you'll never have enough. And those you do have eventually rust, rot, break, crash, or get hopelessly scratched up. Athletes get old and frail, beauty queens get old and wrinkled, and teachers get old and mindless. Loved ones can leave you, disrespect you, divorce you, or die when you're least prepared for it. Life is frightfully insecure if it is based on such things as possessions, performance, and relationships with other people.

So, where can you find life? In the ultimate friend. We need a friend who knows all about us, yet loves us just the way we are—so we know that friend's opinion of us will never change. We need a friend who is genuinely valuable (a superstar) and who lives forever—so we won't be bereaved by death. If we could find such a friend, we could have a strong sense of self-worth and meaning in our lives. And that sense of self-worth wouldn't be hostage to the ups and downs of the stock market, the highs and lows of our daily performance, or the moods and whims of our everyday friends and relatives.

I have good news for you. Such a friend lives. His name is Jesus. He is worth the whole universe, yet He knows all about us and loves us as we are. And He will never die, so we can know that in Him our value is secure throughout eternity. To have Jesus is to have life, even in poverty, sickness, and bereavement. To know Jesus the way John knew Jesus is to understand why the martyrs chose to die rather than reject Him—they'd discovered that life without Jesus just wasn't worth living.

This is not to imply that possessions, performance, and people have no valid role in life. We need possessions in order to live. Performance is all about making a difference in the world. And our relationships with people are deeply enjoyable. All these are an important part of life. But when we base our life on them instead of on God, we find that they are not stable grounds for self-worth and meaning. When our lives are centered in God, on the other hand, these other values of our lives take their appropriate place.

Satan tempts us to seek life apart from our relationship with God. He tempts us to seek life in things that cannot satisfy, in performance that is erratic, and in relationships that are often transitory and problematic. But we can find true life only in God through Jesus Christ.

Foretastes of the Cross

We noticed at the beginning of this chapter that the two "acted parables" in the second chapter of the Gospel of John contain foretastes of the Cross. In the wedding story, such foretastes of the Cross include "the third day," "woman," "hour," "wine," and "glory." This theme of the Cross continues in the episode about the cleansing of the temple. Jesus replaces the sacrificial animals and the temple itself with His own body (John 2:19-21). When Jesus said, "Destroy this temple, and I will raise it again in three days," He was clearly referring to His death on the cross and the resurrection that would follow.

It is the Cross that establishes the value of a human being. The Creator of the universe is more valuable than everything and everyone in the universe, including all the toys and all the great athletes, political figures, and movie stars that we're tempted to worship. His decision to die for you and me placed an infinite value on our lives. If we're that valuable to the greatest Person in the universe, then it doesn't matter whether we're rich or poor, great or small, famous or ordinary, and it doesn't matter what anyone else thinks of us. We *are* truly valuable in Christ. And the Cross is the place where that value is demonstrated without question.

No wonder Paul said, "May I never boast except in the cross of our Lord Jesus Christ, through which the world has been crucified to me, and I to the world" (Gal. 6:14). Paul could turn his back on the allurements of the world—its possessions, performance, and people—because he had found meaning and value in something far more stable and satisfying: the cross of Jesus Christ. "At the foot of the cross, remembering that for one sinner Christ would have laid down His life, you may estimate the value of a soul."[2] That same cross is a central theme of the Gospel of John.

1. See Ellen G. White, *The Desire of Ages* (Nampa, Idaho: Pacific Press, 1940), 146; hereinafter *The Desire of Ages*.
2. Ellen G. White, *Christ's Object Lessons* (Hagerstown, Md.: Review and Herald, 1941), 196.

CHAPTER

Grace Is All-Inclusive

John 2:23–4:42

"Oh, no!" Samantha* said to herself as she approached the well with an empty jug on her head. "A Jew, of all people!" The Jew was sitting near her destination, tired, dirty, and all alone.

"Won't I ever get any peace?" Samantha groaned.

She already knew the answer to that question. No, she would never have any peace in this life. Not only was she a Samaritan, part of a small, despised minority, but she was also a dirty, defiled, hopeless sinner. Five different men had been attracted to her, married her, and then discarded her like a smelly rag.

She thought for a minute about the lazy lout back home who shared her bed and her dinner table but could never earn her respect. She had enough self-respect not to marry a loser like that. Yet she couldn't bring herself to kick him out of the house. What

---

* We don't know her name.

did that make her? A loser among losers? A loser, that's what she was—a loser attracted to other losers. Hopeless.

That's why she was approaching the well at high noon, sweating in the heat of the day. In the morning and evening there would be lots of women at the well. Lots of talk. Lots of laughter. Great gossip. But then the stony silence when she showed up. Everyone looking the other way. Some spitting on the ground near her feet, once or twice even in her face. They hated her for the marriages she had ruined, the husbands she had "stolen," the threat to their homes that they continued to see in her. No, she didn't need any more rejection. She had learned to come to the well at times when no one else was there.

And now this Jew was sitting there. No way to avoid Him. *What's the matter with those Jews, anyway?* she thought. *They and their silly little temple back in Jerusalem. Don't they know that Shechem* * *is the real holy city? Don't they know their own sacred writings? Don't they know that Abraham built his first altar here? Don't they know that Abraham sacrificed his son Isaac here on Mount Gerizim?* † *That Jacob settled here when he returned from Mesopotamia and dug this well? Don't they know that the Israelites had their first worship service here and not in Jerusalem? Don't they know that Jerusalem remained in pagan hands for nearly a thousand years after Abraham? We are the real people of God, not them. Boy, am I glad I'm not a Jew. Then I'd* really *be a loser!*

Her confused thoughts began running together, and she decided to act as if the Jewish Stranger were not there. No Jew would want to talk to her anyway. Especially not one who knew anything about her past! Maybe she could just sneak up to the well, fill her jug, and make a quick getaway before He said anything. It would probably work.

---

* The ancient name of Sychar, where Jacob's well was located.

† A Samaritan tradition not confirmed in our Hebrew Old Testament.

As quietly as possible, she let down the bucket, heard the distant sound of splashing water, and filled her jug. She raised the jug to her head and turned to leave. His voice broke through the turmoil in her mind. "Would you give Me a drink?"

Jesus Knows

In a way, the story of the Samaritan woman really begins with John 2:23-25. This passage sets the stage for Jesus' encounters with Nicodemus (3:1-21) and, later, the Samaritan woman (4:7-42). In John 2:23-25 some people express a superficial faith in Jesus that is based upon miracles but does not result in a saving relationship with Him. Jesus sees right through their profession of faith and discerns their real motives. People sometimes think that if they could see miracles, they would have more faith. But miracles are no cure for superficial faith. They can even get in the way of true faith, hindering us from perceiving the deeper aspects of a relationship with Jesus.

We may tremble at first when we realize that Jesus knows absolutely everything about us. But there's a bright side to consider: If He knows all about us, He knows how to strengthen our faith. During our devotions He can impress us with the insights we need to deepen our relationship with Him. And we don't need to fear confessing our sins to Him—because He already knows, there's nothing to hide. There's no danger in being honest. We are free to become ourselves.

The story is told that when Martin Luther was in exile at Wartburg Castle, the devil tried to discourage him by confronting him with a list of his sins. Luther retorted to the devil, "You'd better work a little harder; that list isn't very complete." The devil returned later with a longer list. Luther responded, "That's better, but it still isn't complete." So, the devil returned still later with a really long list. Luther checked it over. "Yes, I think you have them all now," he said. "Now let me tell you something: The blood of Jesus cleanses from all sin, so get out of here!" Then he picked up a bottle of ink and threw it at the devil. Tourists today can still see the ink stain where the bottle smashed against the wall. (Rumor has it that the castle staff touches up the stain now and then.)

There is freedom and joy in a relationship with someone who knows all about you and loves you just the same. That is the kind of relationship we can have with Jesus.

He Came by Night

As we noted earlier, in the Gospel of John, Jesus doesn't speak in parables. Instead, John tells actual events in Jesus' ministry in such a way that they become acted parables of the spiritual realities Jesus taught. In Nicodemus, for example, we see a living example of a person whose faith was inadequate because it was based merely on miraculous signs (as expressed in John 2:23-25). He comes to Jesus late in the evening of the same day in which Jesus cleansed the temple (2:13-22).

The name *Nicodemus* means "leader of the people." Nicodemus was undoubtedly a pious man, an example of the very best that Judaism could offer. He was a Pharisee, which means that he took the Scriptures and his faith very seriously. He was a member of the Sanhedrin, the Jewish ruling council, and quite well educated. (Jesus called him "the" teacher of Israel, [John 3:10].) So, he must have been a major figure within the Jewish faith. His great learning and high position made it difficult for him to think new thoughts. But his night visit was as bold as it was timid—Nicodemus had a lot to lose in identifying with Jesus.

The story of Nicodemus opens with a conjunction that expresses continuation rather than a clean break. (See John 3:1, where it is helpfully translated "now" in the NIV and many other versions.) Nicodemus's opening comment further underlines the relationship between the story about him and the previous section. Nicodemus's words, "We know" (3:2), indicate that he speaks for others; he is a representative figure. In this story Nicodemus represents those in the previous passage who saw what Jesus did in the temple, but whose faith was still inadequate.

An interesting word usage at the beginning of verse 2 playfully expresses this inadequate faith of Nicodemus. Greek words can express three different aspects of time: a point in time, duration of time, or quality of time. The Greek word for "night" in this verse comes in a form that emphasizes not so much the dark portion of the daily cycle, but darkness as a quality—the darkness in Nicodemus's soul when he came to Jesus. The Savior's knowledge of the state of Nicodemus's heart triggered the "new birth" challenge that He set before him.

So, the Nicodemus story continues the themes emphasized in chapter two. As in 2:23-25, Jesus knows the secrets of the heart (3:3). He wants Nicodemus to understand that people don't enter the kingdom of God by being born into a particular race or nation, that it's a matter of personal decision. Jesus knows all about Nicodemus, and He replaces Nicodemus's religious ideas with a radical new birth (3:5-8). As in chapter two, the Cross is the grounds for everything that Jesus offers (3:14-17).

Born of Water

A major issue regarding the Nicodemus story is the meaning of the water Jesus spoke of in John 3:5. Jesus said, "Unless a man is born of water and the Spirit, he cannot enter the kingdom of God." Was Jesus referring to the water of baptism, as many have thought, or to something else?

The rabbis taught that babies were made of the water in their mother's uterus. They thought that the water that pours out at birth is the residue left over from the development process. If Jesus had this kind of water in mind, He was saying, "To get into the kingdom of God, you need to be born twice, once physically by your birth mother, and the second time spiritually by the Holy Spirit."

There are significant arguments in favor of this interpretation. Until the time of John the Baptist, only Gentile proselytes were baptized. Jews generally did not feel the need to be baptized. One could question, then, whether Nicodemus could possibly have understood Jesus to be talking about baptism. And in John 2:6, water represented the ritualistic forms of religion that Jesus sought to replace. So, to understand the water of John 3:5 to be birth water would continue the replacement theme begun in John 2.

But strong arguments can also be made that Jesus was referring to baptism. If Nicodemus had been part of the delegation of Pharisees that questioned John the Baptist (1:24-28), he might easily have understood Jesus to be saying, "You need to be baptized not only in water but also in the Spirit." Water and Spirit are closely related in Jesus' teaching in John 4:10-14, 23-24; 7:37-39. Cleansing by water and by the Spirit were live concepts in the background of first-century Judaism (see Ezek. 36:25-27; 1 QS [Qumran *Community Rule*] 3:6-9). The Jews believed that a cleansing of Israel in water and Spirit was to precede the coming of the Messiah (see the apocryphal book Psalms of Solomon 18:5, 6). And the concept of being "born from above" is related to the baptism that John the Baptist preached in John 3:22-36. So it is consistent with the context to see in Jesus' statement a reference to baptism both by water and by Spirit.

In either case, the startling concept that Jesus communicated to Nicodemus is that people don't enter the kingdom of God by being born into a particular race or nation; entrance there is a matter of personal decision. To enter it, one must make a spiritual commitment to a new birth, to a changed life. The change is not effected by human effort, however; it comes by the work of the Spirit, which cannot be fully comprehended yet is real (3:8).

What happens to a person who is born again? Verse 8 contains an astonishing statement: "The wind blows wherever it pleases. You hear its sound, but you cannot tell where it comes from or where it is going. So it is with everyone born of the Spirit." The new birth makes one like the Holy Spirit, who blows wherever He wishes. Rather than becoming predictable, like manufactured cookies, Christians energized by the new birth become unpredictable. Nicodemus and the Pharisees preferred a carefully controlled religion in which everyone observed methodical rituals. But the energy of the Spirit brings out the true, God-given uniqueness of all who are born again. In Christ, and through the work of the Spirit, we become our true selves—creative and unique, just like the Spirit.

We see the same uniqueness in Jesus. The Gospel of John pictures Jesus as constantly catching people by surprise. He tells old men to be born again. He speaks to Samaritans. He refuses to be bound by family pressures (John 2:4; 7:1-10). People never know what He will do or say next (John 7:8-11; 8:1-11; 10:24; 11:55-57). We must never let our fear of uniqueness blind us to the working of the Spirit.

Nicodemus asked how such a transformation could possibly take place (3:9). Jesus replied that no human being could answer that question, even if that person could ascend to heaven (3:11-13). The answer will come only from One whose essential nature belongs in heaven and who has come down as the Son of Man to disclose the realities of heaven (3:13).

Then Jesus proceeded to answer Nicodemus's question. The key to the new birth is the lifting up of the Son of Man (3:14, 15; 7:39). It is the Cross, not human effort, that makes the new birth possible (cp. 1:12, 13). Apparently, the Pharisees didn't believe in a suffering and dying Messiah. In 3:14, 15, then, Jesus tells Nicodemus the one thing that Pharisees needed to know in order to enter the kingdom of God.

Jesus compared the Cross to the serpent that Moses lifted up in the wilderness (3:14, 15; cp. Num. 21:4-9). It is an apt comparison. In both cases God provided the remedy, which looked strikingly like the disease. In both cases the remedy was conspicuously displayed. In both cases it was by looking to the remedy that people were cured. And in both cases the consequences of disobedience were the same. The Cross is a life-and-death matter to human beings.

She Came by Day

The Nicodemus story is about a man who came to Jesus at night. John 4 tells the story of a woman who came to Jesus at midday. She came at the sixth hour, noon—the same time of day when Jesus was condemned to the cross, where He also expressed thirst (19:14, 28). Noon was not the usual time for fetching water in Palestine. Women preferred the cooler hours around sunrise and sunset. The time of this woman's arrival, then, probably indicates that she was an outcast in her own town, no doubt due to her marital history and status (4:17, 18).

There were three strikes against this woman's developing a relationship with Jesus. She was a woman in a public place, and Jewish men didn't speak to women in public places. She was a member of a hated race. And she was "living in sin." So, no respectable Jewish man would be caught speaking to her. But Jesus reached across all the barriers in order to provide for her the living water that He had come to give.

Jesus used her expression of interest in the living water (4:15) to confront her with the realities of her life (vs. 16-18). Jesus knew all about her (cf. 2:23-25), and He exposed her evil deeds (cf. 3:20). She tried changing the subject in order to buy time to think (4:19, 20), but soon confessed and accepted Jesus (vs. 29, 42).

The openness with which Jesus confessed His messiahship to this woman is breathtakingly unique to this Gospel (4:26). Apparently, the Samaritan community was a place where Jesus could reveal Himself more openly than He did among the Jews. The Jews expected a military and political Messiah. They denied the concept of a suffering and dying Messiah. So, if Jesus were to assert among the Jews that He was the Messiah, it would result only in misunderstanding.

The Samaritans, on the other hand, knew something right about the Messiah. Since they acknowledged only the five books of Moses as Scripture, their main text regarding the Messiah was Deuteronomy 18:15-18, which says that He would be a prophet like Moses. From this they concluded that the Messiah would be a reformer who would teach them a better way of worship. So, when Jesus talked about a better way of worship, the woman immediately thought of the Messiah (4:23-25). Jesus reinforced the Samaritans' correct understanding by revealing Himself openly to them in a way that He never did among the Jews.

Nic and Sam: Opposites Attract

It is said that in relationships, opposites attract. John portrayed Nicodemus and the Samaritan woman as polar opposites. So, if the above maxim is true, Nicodemus and the Samaritan woman might have found each other quite attractive had they had the opportunity to meet. Note the following inverse parallels: Nicodemus was a man; the Samaritan, a woman. He was a Jew, a Pharisee no less; she was a despised Samaritan. He came to Jesus by night; she, at noon. He was rich (John 19:39); she was poor (or she wouldn't have been fetching her own water). He was highly educated ("the" teacher of Israel—John 3:10); she was illiterate (a woman in first-century Palestine). He was pious (a Pharisee); she was an adulteress. He was highly respected; she was despised and rejected, even by her own Samaritan neighbors. He has a great name, known from ancient writings outside the Bible; she is anonymous. He lived in the holy city, Jerusalem; she lived in Sychar (which means "drunkenness"). He was open to believe, yet slow to accept; she was suspicious at first, yet quick to embrace Jesus when she realized who He is.

In these two stories we once again see an acted parable that unfolds the reality of John 3:16. God sent His Son so that "whoever believes" might have eternal life. In Nicodemus and the Samaritan woman we see the opposite extremes of that "whoever." No matter who you are, no matter what you've done, no matter what your pedigree, no matter how others treat you, Jesus exhibits a glorious lack of prejudice. Whoever will may come. There are no conditions of race, religion, sex, custom, wealth, performance, or personal appearance. All are welcome to receive Him. He is truly the "Savior of the world" (John 4:42).

CHAPTER 5

The Struggle to Be Real

John 4:43-54

What a difference a day makes! The sky was bluer, the grass was greener, everyone he passed on the road seemed friendlier— life was suddenly good, very good. But the day had started very differently.

Basilico* had awakened in Capernaum that morning to the realization that unless drastic measures were taken, his son would die. The boy had been ill for several weeks now, and it was clear that his bodily systems were in the last stages of a bitter struggle for life.

Basilico loved his son and longed to do something to help. He remembered that a few months before, Jesus had lived in his village and had healed many people. But now Jesus had taken a long trip south. Would He come back in time? Would He be able to do anything if He did return? If He were really a prophet, as people

---

*We don't know his real name; *Basilico* means "royal official" in Greek. The man was a bureaucrat in the government of Galilee, serving under one of the Herods.

said, He must have known that Basilico's son might die in His absence. Why, then, did He leave? But what if He didn't know? What if His miracles were a fraud? What if they were from Satan? Basilico was confused, but he was running out of options.

Just when all seemed lost, word came that Jesus had returned to Galilee and was visiting Cana. Confusion turned to hope. Nothing else had worked. Getting Jesus to come to Capernaum seemed worth a try. But he'd have to hike to Cana, which was 16 miles and 1,700 feet of altitude away—a stiff hike in anybody's book. And after all that hiking, he'd have to talk Jesus into returning with him that same day.

He set out at six in the morning to the sound of his son's gasping breath and hacking cough. There was no time to lose! Driven by hope, Basilico attained a pace he could never have sustained otherwise. Around noon he stopped briefly to rest, having climbed to within a couple miles of Cana. He pondered how he ought to approach Jesus when he found Him. It simply would not do for Jesus to know that he had doubts. He must approach Jesus in full confidence that He could heal his son. . . .

Developing Faith

It is likely that Jesus and the royal official knew each other well. After all, they spent at least several months as fellow citizens in the same small village* (John 2:12; 4:46). In the Gospel of John, however, knowing Jesus in the flesh often led to doubt rather than to faith. Jesus' initial response (4:48) indicates that this man, like Nicodemus before him, was an example of inadequate faith. It seems that the Galileans on the whole welcomed Jesus outwardly but did not really believe in Him (4:43-45). They were quick to be awed by miracles and spectacular works, but they were slow to

---

*Ancient Capernaum was not much bigger than a par-three hole on a golf course.

respond to His words. The miracles may actually have become stumbling blocks on the way to a true appreciation of Jesus.

A Galilean himself, the royal official was confronted by the reality of his partial, inadequate faith. He didn't rely on the naked word of Jesus, but required physical evidence before he would believe. He was startled to discover that he couldn't hide his unbelief from Jesus. Realizing that he might lose all on account of unbelief, he finally threw himself at Jesus' feet in desperation. Surely if Jesus could read the secrets of his heart (2:23-25), He could do whatever He wanted with the man's request.

Then Jesus shocked the man by saying that He didn't need to travel to Capernaum; He could heal at a great distance. This claim was the final piece that brought faith to the royal official. But belief brought with it a test. Would he act on this newfound faith? Would he head home believing that his son would live, or would he continue to beg Jesus to come home and touch the sick boy?

The man's actions demonstrated his newfound faith. If he had hurried downhill, he could have made it back to Capernaum that night. Instead, he took the scenic route. He stopped to smell the flowers and talk to people. He spent the night in a motel and slept in. He took so long going home that the family sent servants to look for him! So the man not only headed home alone at Jesus' command, he did so in a manner that indicated he had fully accepted Jesus' word. Those who believe, act; the evidence of faith is action.

How can we apply this faith lesson to our lives today? How can we receive answers to our requests, just like the man from Capernaum did? The story suggests four steps: *(1) Know that you have a problem.* This is not as simple as it sounds—I'll discuss it further in the last part of this chapter. *(2) Take your problem to Jesus.* We must take our problem to Him in prayer. And we must not fear to share it with a prayer partner or a prayer group. *(3) Receive the word that your need has been met.* The words of Jesus to us are found in the Bible. If we want to hear that word, we need to know the Word. *(4) Speak and act God's answer.* It is not enough simply to hear the word. God's word becomes real to us when we *act* on it and when we *tell others* about our faith. Genuine belief results in corresponding action.

But what if we are like the royal official? What if our belief is mixed with unbelief? What if we have doubts? This story suggests that we need to confront the doubts with words of faith and with action. Take God at His word. *Do* what the Bible says, and faith will come. When we talk faith, we will have *more* faith.[1]

Mrs. Highhouse learned the above steps one Sabbath. Wanting a deeper relationship with Jesus, she decided to spend time every morning receiving His words through the study of the Bible. She committed herself to getting up early on Sunday and studying the book of Romans with the help of Martin Luther's commentary. She acted by laying out her Bible and Luther's book on her study desk Saturday night.

Sunday morning she awoke with a splitting headache, unable to study. She prayed, "Lord, I know You want me to spend time with You this morning, so please take the headache away." She waited ten minutes and nothing happened. She prayed again and nothing happened. Then she remembered step four: "Speak and act God's answer." So she told God, "I know You want me to spend time with You, so I will do my best. The headache is Your problem." She began to study, headache and all. About ten minutes later it dawned on her that the headache was gone. That incident had a giant impact on her faith.

Steps to Authenticity

The royal official didn't know the depths of his unbelief until Jesus confronted him directly. Like him, we too are often unaware of our sinfulness and unbelief. We act out the truth of Jeremiah 17:9: "The heart is deceitful above all things." How can we bring a problem to Jesus when our heart is deceiving us, when we don't even know that we have a problem? *How can we "get real" with God?*

1. Spend time with the Word of God. The Bible aids our search for authenticity by affirming our value before God. As you read, look for the many ways that the gospel comes through. Mark the passages that reveal how much God values us. Many of us have been raised in a legalistic setting in which the gospel was affirmed in speech, but was made unbelievable in experience. It is imperative, therefore, that we saturate ourselves in the biblical texts that affirm the gospel until every legalistic doubt in our minds is driven away. Only when we know and understand the gospel will we have the courage to enter into the process of growing self-awareness.

Further help to our search for self-awareness can be found in the Bible's biographies, the stories about the major characters. Scripture portrays character after character authentically: it pictures real people with significant flaws. In fact, many of its characters seem more messed up than you or I am. Yet God used them in spite of their flaws. This characteristic of the Bible is powerfully described in one of the most remarkable passages in Ellen White's writings, volume 4, pages 9-11, of *Testimonies for the Church.*

The Bible is authentic. Even in translation, 2 Samuel will knock your socks off. As far as Hollywood goes, 2 Samuel is definitely R-rated. (R-rated movies are usually full of sex and violence.) But in the Bible, unlike in Hollywood, the sex and violence function to show us the folly of a life apart from God and the pain that comes when we violate the laws of our being. They are there to encourage us that, like David, we can break away from the darkness to a better way of life. An honest reading of the Bible encourages authenticity and gives us the courage to confess our sins. Since God could accept David, there's hope that He'll accept us, too.

2. Practice authentic prayer. A crucial companion to authentic Bible study is authentic prayer. What I mean by authentic prayer is prayer that is directed toward God in full commitment. It is wholehearted, whole-souled immersion in the prayer experience. Authentic prayer says, "I want the truth, no matter what the cost." When we seek truth in the Bible, we need to allow God to open us up to His Spirit, to make us willing to know the truth, to accept the truth, and to follow the truth wherever it leads. When you tell God, "I want the truth no matter what the cost," you will receive it, but you will also pay the cost. Truth can cost you your family, your job, your reputation. It can even cost you your life. Do you want to know the truth that much? If you do, God will give it to you.

In a previous book, *Present Truth in the Real World,*[2] I told about a time when I was wrestling to know God's will in my life. I was lying face down on a hardwood floor in Brooklyn. I didn't know what to do. Finally, in desperation I cried out to God, "I want the truth, the whole truth, and nothing but the truth, and I don't care what it costs me!" And God gave me what I needed. My life has never been the same.

But wanting the truth no matter what the cost turned out to be only the first step in authentic prayer. I have learned to go to an even deeper level of prayer. One could call this deeper level *Authentic Prayer II: The Sequel!* It goes something like this: "Lord, I want the truth *about myself* no matter what the cost."

Truth can be very abstract. It can be a correct understanding of all the beasts of Revelation. Having a correct understanding can be very satisfying, but that kind of truth can become a substitute for a more practical kind. Knowing the truth about ourselves differs greatly from knowing truth in the abstract. It comes very, very close to home. It is knowing ourselves the way some other people know us. So, you could pray for this kind of truth like this: "Lord, help me to see myself as other people see me. Help me to get the kind of understanding about myself that other people have." The beautiful thing about God is that He loves to share truth with anyone who's willing to listen. If you're willing to pay the cost, you'll know the truth about yourself to the degree that you are ready for it.

3. Use various types of journaling. The practice of journaling is a close companion to authentic prayer. God uses the process of journaling to probe the depths of our being in ways that nothing else can. We can use journaling to pray, to record God's answers to prayer, and to take note of the various ways in which God's power has been at work in our life. Journaling encourages authenticity; you'll find it particularly helpful to invite God to probe whatever area of your life He wishes to examine and to expose you to it in writing! Many of the greatest Christians of all time, including Ellen White, practiced journaling as a tool of self-awareness. (For a detailed description of different types of journaling, see my book *Knowing God in the Real World.*[3])

4. Accountability. The deepest level on the journey toward authenticity is accountability. Self-deception is deep-rooted enough in all of us that it is intertwined even into our prayer lives and our Bible study. Sometimes God can break through to us only through another human being.

> There are souls perplexed with doubt, burdened with infirmities, weak in faith, and unable to grasp the Unseen; but a friend whom they can see, coming to them in Christ's

stead, can be a connecting link to fasten their trembling faith upon Christ.[4]

Being accountable means allowing others to help us keep watch over ourselves. There are a number of ways that we can take advantage of this. One way is through a sharing group like Alcoholics Anonymous or a "cell church," where one is penalized only for being inauthentic. Everybody is required to tell the truth and is accepted in their telling of it. As you hear somebody else telling the truth about themselves, you connect with what they are saying and realize that you have some of those same faults yourself. You recognize yourself in the confession of another. In an atmosphere where people are confessing their sins, you have the courage to confess your own.

Related to this concept of small groups is an insight from Seventh-day Adventist history that a friend suggested to me. Many of the *Testimonies for the Church* read as if they were the journals of the people they were written to. In the *Testimonies,* God was offering a unique path to authenticity, telling people truths about themselves that they had failed to discover on their own. Perhaps the goal of these *Testimonies* is not so much to provide unbending rules for all who read them as it is to do the work of a small group in the readers' own quest for accountability. Rightly handled, the *Testimonies* can open up windows into our depravity, to which we can then apply the gospel for forgiveness and healing.

I have an even scarier suggestion for the few and the brave. Find a hard-nosed friend who cares deeply about you—someone who would never want to see you hurt. Tell this friend, "If you knew that I wouldn't get mad and take it out on you later, what is there about me that you would tell me? What problems do you see in my relationship with God? How do I come across to other people?"

What if you don't have any close friends? What if there is no one on this earth whom you would trust with the deepest anguish of your heart? Even if this is your situation, you can obtain the benefit of accountability. Find a good Christian counselor to help you. Counselors are trained to help people open up and discover the deep truth about themselves. They're trained to be good listeners. Often, they can detect when you are playing games of self-deception. They're trained to offer the kind of accountability we need in the context of confidentiality. While I have found counseling helpful at various stages of my life, it is particularly critical for those who have nowhere else to turn. Life is too short to waste living inauthentically.

People today hunger for a faith that is real, a faith that makes a difference in everyday life. We can find such a faith when we open ourselves to God in the context of a community of people who are together on a journey toward God in Jesus Christ. The grace and kindness we find in Jesus through the gospel gives us the courage to face the truth about ourselves. We can also take courage that the same prophet who warned us about the deceitfulness of our hearts (Jer. 17:9) also conveyed our Lord's promise: "You will seek me and find me when you seek me with all your heart" (Jer. 29:13).

---

1. See Ellen G. White, *The Ministry of Healing* (Nampa, Idaho: Pacific Press, 1942), 251–253; hereinafter, *The Ministry of Healing.*

2. Jon Paulien, *Present Truth in the Real World* (Nampa, Idaho: Pacific Press, 1993).

3. Jon Paulien, *Knowing God in the Real World* (Nampa, Idaho: Pacific Press, 2001).

4. *The Desire of Ages,* 297.

CHAPTER 6

Putting the Past Behind You

John 5:1-47

What is life anyway? How would I know, I never had one! All I do is lie around waiting for something to happen, but it never does, at least not for me. I have no friends. I guess I never had any friends, at least not since this happened to me. I have no money. I can't work. I'm bored. I have no life! And I know in my heart of hearts that nothing will ever change. Then why am I here?

The crippled man lay on a mat beside a pool in Jerusalem. Rumor had it that every so often an angel came down and stirred the waters of the pool, and the first one into the pool after the water was stirred would be cured of whatever disease he or she had. Huge crowds came to be healed, so much so that the crippled man often couldn't even see the pool from where he lay. The least trembling of the water resulted in such a stampede that some had been trampled to death in the process. So for years now he watched the water, waiting for a chance to be healed. But whenever the water was troubled, someone less sick than he would be in first. It was hopeless. As the years went by the man's eyes glazed over in despair more and more often. The paralysis of body became a paralysis of mind.

As time dragged on, he sometimes allowed himself a few moments of regret. As a young man, he had engaged in some very risky behaviors—sin the rabbis called it. They had warned him that sin would lead to sickness and death, and in his case it had—a living death. What was it that had driven him to sin even when he had tried to stop? What kind of emptiness had pushed him to continue in destructive behaviors? Had he known the consequences of his sins, would he have quit in time? Or was he just doomed to this kind of existence? Thirty-eight years of suffering. Was it fair? Did he really deserve this?

Even worse than the paralysis, however, was the rejection. Because his sickness was the consequence of his sins, most people, especially the religious people, had rejected him. He was abandoned to his fate—left all alone with his thoughts, and his thoughts were no fun at all.

Suddenly a kind face bent over him and broke through his glazed stare. He saw in that face the compassion of a Man who knew what it was like to suffer rejection. He saw interest and concern. The Man said, "Do you want to get well?"

What kind of question is that? the crippled man thought, *Do I want to get well? Does a drowning man want air? Does a pig like mud? Does a Pharisee want publicity? Does a Roman want power? Do I want to get well? Who is this guy, anyway?*

The House of Mercy

Archaeologists have unearthed the pool of Bethesda in Jerusalem. It lay just north of the temple complex. It was laid out in an uneven rectangle (a trapezoid) about 200 feet wide and 300 feet long, 40 feet deep at the deepest point, hewn entirely out of rock. The pool was surrounded by colonnades on all four sides and was divided into two parts by a colonnade in the center, confirming the biblical record that the pool had five colonnades (John 5:2). The pool's structure was Hellenistic (Greek) in origin; it may have originally been a temple in honor of the Greek god of healing, Asclepius. The pool was fed below ground by an intermittent stream, which may explain the movement of the waters. With its Hellenistic edifice, the pool probably attracted people with a wide mix of beliefs, all hoping to find restoration from the ailments of human life.

The name *Bethesda* meant "house of mercy," but the hundreds who sought healing there found little mercy. Although the King James Bible states that an angel of the Lord stirred the healing waters, the older biblical manuscripts leave out that element of the story.* It would certainly have been strange for God to arrange a healing mechanism that favored the least sick over the truly needy. What we know for sure is that in this story Jesus shows mercy at the place where people looked for mercy.

Implications of the Story

Once again we discover that the stories in the Gospel of John serve as acted parables of who Jesus is and what He's like. Several aspects of this story cry out for attention. First of all, Jesus healed the man arbitrarily. He picked one man out of a whole crowd of people: a man who hadn't sought Jesus out, a man who didn't even know Him, a man who expressed no faith in Him before being healed. This reminds me of so many people who have told me that at a decisive point in their lives, they felt God's hand in ways they hadn't asked for and didn't deserve. God does things such as this, not to excuse sin, but so we can experience His grace and thereby gain courage to deal with sin.

---

*See the explanation in *The Desire of Ages,* 201.

53

A second startling aspect to the story is that Jesus chose to heal the man on the Sabbath. The rabbis allowed for special acts on the Sabbath in emergencies, but this was no emergency. After all, the man had been crippled for thirty-eight years—surely a day or two's delay for the sake of the Sabbath would not have made a major difference. So Jesus was deliberately making a point here. "It is lawful to do good on the Sabbath," Jesus had said (Matt. 12:12). Here, Jesus was carrying out what He taught. The Sabbath is a day when doing good is particularly appropriate. When we do good deeds on the Sabbath, we model our actions on those that God does on this day.

Most interesting of all, however, is the implication of verse 14. When Jesus told the man to "stop sinning," He implied, first of all, that the man's illness was caused by sin in some sense. Continued sin might result in a relapse of the paralysis. But there is an even deeper element here. The form of the word translated "sinning" is extremely continuous. This implies that the man had somehow been continuing in sin, even in a paralyzed state. What kind of sin was Jesus talking about? A paralyzed man cannot rob banks, commit adultery, or kill anyone. Jesus must have been referring to sin of the mind. The man's physical illness had resulted from unhealthful mental processes. The physical healing of the invalid was only the tip of the iceberg. Jesus was interested in healing the whole person.

The hurts of the past include not only physical injuries but emotional, spiritual, and psychological wounds. A relationship with Jesus can and should address all these. All other things being equal, a genuine walk with Jesus brightens the facial expressions, soothes the emotions, warms the heart, and brings renewed energy to the body. This is why Seventh-day Adventist Christianity is so concerned with things such as diet, exercise, and attitude. Genuine faith involves every part of life—mental, physical, and emotional, as well as spiritual.

Dealing With Emotional Pain

Having said this, most Christians readily acknowledge that their inner life, particularly the emotional aspect, remains quite unstable even after conversion. The "old nature" rises up again and again to trouble and to torment. Like everyone else, Christians have to struggle with unhappy memories, flashes of anger, and unmentionable thoughts. Jesus cares at least as much about the inner life as He does about the outward circumstances.

Unwelcome thoughts and emotions can revolve around two types of past event: things we have done and things that have been done to us. Things we have done cause feelings of remorse, regret, and failure. Memories of failure can cause us to become timid and cautious, on the one hand ("I never do anything right") or reckless on the other ("It doesn't matter what I do"). Things others have done to us can cause feelings of anger, grief, and deep resentment. All the above emotions came together as a result of a deep emotional wound that I experienced as a teen.

When I was in academy, my hero was the Bible teacher. I wanted above all else to be like him when I grew up. It just so happens that as a senior, I was the quarterback on the best flag-ball team in the school. That meant that I had the dubious privilege of refereeing games in which I was not playing.

One day I refereed a game in which the Bible teacher had a rooting interest. Things turned sour almost from the first snap from center. "That was a stupid call! What's the matter? Are you blind or something? How much is the other team paying you?" Similar comments shouted from the sideline poured out of his mouth for nearly an hour. I bravely acted as though I didn't hear and continued doing my best.

Finally I followed a power sweep that ended directly in front of the Bible teacher along the sideline. I was on top of the play and made the call as I saw it. He exploded in my face. "I can't believe that call! You are ridiculous! I have never seen such a sorry display of refereeing in all my life!" Struggling to control my emotions, I picked up the football and walked over to the Bible teacher and with a trembling voice said, "I'm sorry. I'm doing the best I can." He looked me in the eye and said with a tone of contempt, "Your best isn't good enough!"

I threw the finest spiral in all my years as a quarterback. It landed on the roof of a four-story building near the playing field. I walked off the field to the sound of the gym teacher canceling the entire flag-ball season. I found the deepest, darkest corner of that academy and cried for two hours. No one could stop me. For months I waited to hear an apology but never received one. Ten years later I still found it difficult to tell this story without tears.

Why did I cry? Because when my personal hero told me that my best wasn't good enough, I lost all hope. I believed that my best would *never* be good enough. I learned that I could not trust those I cared about the most. The future looked dark and meaningless. I'm thankful that as the years have gone by, I have learned some practical steps by which people can open themselves up to the healing power of Jesus, not just in areas of physical health but also in the emotional areas of their lives. I am slowly learning how to deal with painful memories and deep resentments. I am learning how to put the past behind me and move on.

Virtually everyone has had an experience like the one I had on the flag-football field. Many have had a long string of similar experiences. The crucial issue in emotional healing is the matter of how we can overcome painful memories and emotional wounds. In cases where there has been severe abuse, or a record of extreme violence and/or promiscuity, the process of emotional healing will necessarily be long and complex. But over the years I have learned some strategies that have helped me along the road to recovery. Here's what I've learned.

Putting the Past Behind You

1. Choose healing. Many people prefer being right to being healed. They would rather be bitter and vindictive and enjoy blaming someone else for their troubles than pursue the healing that can come only from forgiveness. That is why people often have to "hit bottom"—in other words, see their lives spiral into total disasters such as divorce or addiction—before they are willing to seek healing change. People rarely recover from emotional pain until they want recovery more than anything else.

2. Look the past in the eye. Face the reality about things you have done or that have been done to you. Seek authentic knowledge about the past. Through prayer, Bible study, journaling, and accountability, seek to sort reality from the swirl of thoughts and emotions related to that reality. Accept responsibility for sinful choices you've made. Acknowledge the pain that comes from things over which you had no control (such as the attitude of a Bible teacher!).

When we're suffering emotional pain because of things that we have done to ourselves or to others (sin), true knowledge of the past leads to confession and repentance. Confession is simply telling the truth about ourselves. When combined with strategy number 8, it can have an incredibly healing effect.

3. Discover your value in God's eyes. It requires tremendous strength of character to look the past in the eye. This is rarely possible outside a relationship in which you know that you are fully accepted no matter what. The gospel teaches us that the most valuable Person in the universe knows all about us, yet loves us with unconditional love. God accepts us as we are. The Cross demonstrates our value to God. We are worth the infinite life of the precious Son of God. And because Jesus will never die again, we can know that He will never abandon us. When we grasp the value we have in God's eyes, we can begin to have the courage to face the past and deal with it.

4. Seek support and guidance. Looking the past in the eye is easier when you have human support as well as divine. Finding friends you can trust is a crucial part of the recovery process. For many, especially the most traumatized, this process may need to begin with a professional counselor—someone who is trained to create a safe environment in which people can talk about the things that trouble them the most. Small groups can be an excellent source of caring friends with listening ears.

5. Tell your story over and over. A crucial part of emotional healing is telling your story over and over. I used my flag-ball story (in places where the Bible teacher was not known) as part of a sermon on self-worth. Time and again I broke down as I told the story. But as time passed, the story became less and less threatening to me, until I could tell it without pain. Another way to process emotional pain is to write out a traumatic story, several times if necessary. You can read the story to yourself and others over and over, allowing you to process the emotions related to the story.

6. Invite Jesus into your traumatic memories. An excellent way to heal a traumatic memory is to invite Jesus into the scene. In your journal or your imagination, consider how the event affected Jesus. What would He say to each person in the scene? How does He feel about you? About the person you hurt or who hurt you? Re-create the memory to include Jesus healing the situation. Make any restitution that He might direct. Accept His forgiveness as needed.

7. Forgive those who have hurt you. When we forgive someone else, it sometimes blesses that person, but it always blesses us. Forgiveness is a choice. We may have to do it several times before it "sticks." Resentment, hatred, and anger may do little damage to the person they're directed against, but they always do heavy damage to the one who experiences them. To forgive is to break the chains of the past. To forgive is to find healing. Jesus longs to help us forgive.

8. Forgive yourself. This is usually harder than forgiving others. Forgive yourself for all the times that you have hurt other people out of your own emotional pain. Make restitution where appropriate. Forgive yourself for judging and condemning those who have hurt you or those you love. When we place ourselves in an atmosphere of confession and repentance, we place ourselves in a position where Jesus can help us forgive ourselves as well as others.

9. Build a new, positive record. The day will come when, though the scar is still there, the pain is gone. We will remember, but it won't hurt anymore. When old records have been closed, it is time to make new records, positive records. Remind yourself how valuable you are in Christ. Practice affirming and encouraging others. Use your story to connect with other hurting people and begin making a positive difference in their lives.

Memorize Scripture to fill your mind with God's wisdom. As you grow, continue the strategies that lead to deeper authenticity. You can work through the above process again as fresh circumstances may require. Putting the past behind you is a lifelong process that Christians sometimes call sanctification.

The Gospel of John assures us that Jesus cares about every aspect of our lives—mental, physical, emotional, and spiritual. We don't have to wait until eternity to enjoy abundant living; we can begin to taste it now (John 10:10). Jesus invites us to be part of the process.

CHAPTER

The Sacred in the Common

John 6:1-71

Jesus and His disciples were exhausted after weeks and weeks of ministry. People needed counseling, physical healing, and sometimes just someone to talk to. Crowds of people. A never-ending stream. While Jesus did most of the work, the disciples were busy too. They organized the people, screened out frivolous requests, helped where they could, and did their best to protect Jesus from over-commitment.

Finally Jesus called the disciples aside and said, "We need a vacation. Let's take off after dark and travel across the lake to that deserted area on the other side." But it was as if they had been set up. Someone raised an alarm as they tried to get into their boat without being noticed. As they cast off from shore they could hear the sounds of townspeople rushing to the docks to follow them in other boats. When morning came on the other side, they discovered that people who didn't own boats had walked around the lake, converging on them from the north.

Then something even worse began to happen. Thousands of people were traveling toward Jerusalem for Passover. As they noticed the crowd gathering around Jesus, many asked what the attraction was and then decided to interrupt their travel for a bit, multiplying the crowd even further. Soon Philip estimated that there were more than ten thousand people trying to get to Jesus.* This was turning into a real zoo!

Just as things were getting out of control Jesus approached Philip. He said, "Philip, between the people who chased after us in the dark and the travelers who aren't going to make the next rest stop, we have a lot of people who are going to be real hungry in a little bit. You used to live around here, how do you suppose we could go about treating everybody to lunch?"

"Are you serious, Master?"

"Maybe," Jesus said with just a bit of a twinkle in His eye.

"There's no way! Even if we could find that much food around here—and I remember the restaurants being few and far between—we'd all have to work for weeks to pay for it! I thought this was supposed to be a vacation. Now what are we going to do?"

Just then Andrew showed up with a little boy whose mom had remembered to pack him a lunch. "Here, Jesus," said the boy. "You can have *my* lunch."

Jesus glanced over the gathering crowd for a minute, and then looked at Philip. The twinkle was still there in His eye. With a wink He said, "You know, I think that might be enough . . ."

Seeing Jesus in the Common

Whenever John referred to the Passover in his Gospel (2:13; 6:4; 13:1), he always alluded to either the Lord's Supper or the

---

* The text says five thousand men; add the women and children who no doubt were there too.

Cross or both. While he did not include an account of the Lord's Supper in his Gospel, he explained its meaning through acted parables in chapter 6. The true meaning of the Passover is to be found in the person of Jesus and in the Supper that only He can provide. So once again Jesus takes something that is good—Passover, in this case—and transforms it into something even better.

It is interesting, however, that both of John's major allusions to the Lord's Supper are found in the context of picnic lunches: this one on a hillside (6:1-13, especially verse 11), the other on a beach (21:1-14). In a sense the Communion service, the dinner table, and a picnic are all alike. Jesus' presence cannot be confined to church buildings where the "right" style of worship services are performed. For those who walk with Jesus, there is a sense in which every meal can become a sacrament, an event in which we experience the real and empowering presence of Jesus.

You see, were it not for the cross of Jesus Christ, there would be no bread, no water, no rain, no life. All these things would have ceased with the entrance of sin. "To the death of Christ we owe even this earthly life. The bread we eat is the purchase of His broken body. The water we drink is bought by His spilled blood. Never one, saint or sinner, eats his daily food, but he is nourished by the body and the blood of Christ. The cross of Calvary is stamped on every loaf. It is reflected in every water spring."[1]

One of the secrets of the devotional life is to learn how to see the presence and the power of Jesus in the common things of everyday life, to sense that He is there with us even though we cannot see, hear, or touch Him. We'll return to this concept at the end of the chapter.

A Walk on the Wild Side

Matthew (14:22-27), Mark (6:45-52), and John (6:16-21) all tell the story of Jesus walking on the water. In all three accounts the disciples get into a boat and head across the Sea of Galilee. This takes place in the evening as it is becoming dark. Jesus is not with them. A strong wind is blowing. The disciples see Jesus walking on the sea and are frightened. He says something like, "It is I; don't be afraid." Then they take Him into the boat. In this story Jesus does something similar to what the God of the Exodus did. To people schooled in the Old Testament, Jesus' ability to walk on water and to control wind and wave was a powerful affirmation of His divinity.

In the story, although the disciples are afraid and despite the mighty works Jesus has done, they don't look to Him for help. When Jesus does appear, they are unprepared for His presence and help. Faith is a mind-set that expects God to be there in every aspect of life. It is the ultimate antidote to fear. The second generation of Christians would see in this story encouragement to expect the presence and help of Jesus even when they felt all alone and forsaken by God. His word is as good as His presence.

Talking to Deaf Ears

It is clear throughout John 6 that the crowds are relating to Jesus on a material level. They are not searching for spiritual food, they want their physical needs to be satisfied. They want to see more miracles like the feeding of the five thousand. Yet despite that awesome event, when the people looked at Jesus, they saw a common, everyday human being like themselves, not Someone who came down from heaven. They couldn't see the sacred shining through the common. The very physical presence of Jesus became a stumbling block to them. This underlines again John's point to the second generation of Christians. We think that those who walked with Jesus had an easier time finding faith than we do, yet Jesus' very physical presence became a stumbling block to them.

John 6:22-59 pictures Jesus trying to direct the crowd's eyes away from His physical presence and the miracles He can do toward spiritual things, the food that endures to eternal life. We do not find life in miracles and in the things of this world (remember our discussion about possessions, performance, and people in chapter three). We find it by accepting the claims that Jesus makes about Himself. Those who believe in Him receive all the evidence that they need; they don't need to see miracles in order to believe. If we talk and act in faith, our faith will grow. But if we wait for God to prove Himself to us, to do something spectacular first, our faith will languish.

The Sacred in the Common

Time and again in his Gospel, John draws symbols from everyday experience, symbols such as bread, water, and light. These symbols help us to connect Jesus' words with our everyday lives. No matter how ordinary our lives may be, our relationship with Jesus will deepen and grow as we learn to remember Him in the course of everything we do. As the Bread of Life, Jesus brings us a taste of eternal life, which makes physical food and drink seem insignificant by comparison.

Have you ever been ravenously hungry or thirsty to the point of desperation? Do you remember what it was like when someone then gave you a cool drink or a slice of French bread slathered with your favorite spread? Jesus wanted memories like that to trigger spiritual meanings, to offer lessons about the life that He came to offer. The message of the Bread of Life sermon is that our need for the spiritual life that Jesus brings is just as desperate as our pangs of physical hunger and thirst. As the body craves food and drink and sunlight, so the soul craves the presence of Jesus. And if we will not allow Jesus to be present, we'll go to all kinds of ridiculous lengths to fill our craving with something else. Inside every human being is a God-sized hole that only Jesus can fill.

How can we satisfy our spiritual craving? We can link the experiences of everyday life with images from the words of Jesus (John 6:63). In Christ, all of life can become a sacrament—we can experience the presence and power of Jesus Christ in the common affairs of everyday life. No matter what we do, we can recall the words Jesus spoke at the inauguration of the Communion service: "This do in remembrance of Me."

When we sit down at a table to eat, we can remember that rain and sunshine and the food production they make possible would all have ceased with sin were it not for the cross of Jesus. When we lift up a glass to drink, we can remember the Water of Life. When we get dressed in the morning, we can think about the robe of Christ's righteousness—His perfect life that offers us a clean record before God. When we relax at home, dry and warm under a sheltering roof, we can rejoice that the righteousness of Christ shelters us from the ultimate consequences of sin. When we go to sleep at night, we can experience a living parable of human frailty, the end of life. Like Jesus on the cross, we can pray, "Father, into Your hands I commit my spirit," knowing we will rise again in the morning, as Jesus did on the first day of the week.

When we attend a wedding or get married ourselves, we can think about the relationship between Christ and the Church (Eph. 5:31, 32). When we get sick, we can think about the One who "took up our infirmities" (Isa. 53:4). When we suffer, we can recall the One who suffered for us (1 Pet. 2:21). And when we come to the end of our lives (if time should last that long), we can celebrate the destruction of our sinful natures, which have tainted our best efforts for Jesus throughout our lives. One of the keys to a living relationship with Jesus is to make all the common events of our lives reminders of His words and actions.

The Story of Judas

A painful sideline to the gospel story is Jesus' traumatic relationship with Judas. Judas is mentioned by name in a total of twenty verses in the four Gospels. Many of these references are directly related to the betrayal story (Matt. 26:14, 25, 47; 27:3; Mark 14:10, 43; Luke 22:3, 47-48; John 13:2, 26, 29). The rest speak to Judas's career as a disciple before Passion Week (Matt. 10:4; Mark 3:19; Luke 6:16; John 6:71; 12:4). The three of these texts outside John's Gospel simply place Judas, with the note, "who betrayed him," on a list of the twelve disciples. So the only significant information about Judas before Passion Week is found in John 6:71 and 12:4.

In John 6:71 we learn that Jesus considered Judas to be "a devil." John 12:4-7 tells us more. There Judas objects to the anointing of Jesus' feet with perfume, arguing that it should have been sold and the money given to the poor. We are told that he was the keeper of the money bag and that he was a thief—he used to help himself to what was in the money bag. Jesus rebukes Judas for objecting to the woman's action.

In Matthew 26, Judas bargains for money in exchange for betraying Jesus. Judas poses as Jesus' friend, betrays Him, and then shows remorse. He returns the money, goes out, and hangs himself. Luke 22 adds the detail that Satan entered into Judas, motivating him to betray Jesus. John 13 has additional detail about the betrayal. Verse 18 suggests that Judas was somehow not chosen by Jesus, and that his betrayal of Jesus was a fulfillment of Scripture. The other disciples clearly knew nothing about his plot (vs. 21-25). Satan enters Judas as Jesus points him out by sharing a piece of dipped bread with him (vs. 26, 27).

In *The Desire of Ages,* Ellen White clarifies and expands on the biblical evidence. She indicates that money had gradually become the ruling principle of Judas's life. Love of money gave Satan an opening by which he could gain control of Judas. He was not chosen by Jesus but joined the disciples in the hope of changing his life. The other disciples held Judas in high esteem, though he despised them. Jesus gave Judas opportunities to understand his selfishness and to change, but he differed with Jesus at a decisive point. He was looking for a more political and economic type of kingdom than the one Jesus offered in John 6. After this event he increasingly expressed private doubts about Jesus, which eventually led to the confrontation at Mary and Martha's house (John 12). Jesus' reproof on that occasion settled Judas in his opposition to Jesus.

Judas reasoned that his betrayal of Jesus would lead to one or the other of two possible good outcomes. If Jesus was right that His crucifixion fulfilled Scripture, then Judas's betrayal wouldn't change anything, and he could keep the money. On the other hand, if Jesus was not supposed to die, He would be forced to deliver Himself, setting in motion the kind of kingdom Judas preferred. Judas would be credited as the one who set in motion the events that led to Jesus' kingship.

Ellen White concluded the sad tale by indicating that Judas's remorse before the priests was played out right in front of Jesus at the trial. Judas begged them to release Jesus, then begged Jesus to free Himself. Seeing all his hopes and dreams going down the drain, Judas went out and hanged himself.

John 6 ends with Judas staying with Jesus for several possible reasons: material gain, political power, and even the hope of a changed life. Sadly, in the end, he got none of them.

---

1. *The Desire of Ages,* 660.

CHAPTER

At the Feast of Tabernacles

John 7:1–10:21

Tuffy was the life of the party. (The Greek word for "blind man" is *tuphlos,* hence "Tuffy.") Although he had been born blind, he had also been born with a keen wit and a sharp tongue. Even before he reached his teen years his quick comebacks and acid humor kept everyone around him constantly in stitches. It wasn't long before he was on everybody's party list. Tuffy was so funny that if he wasn't in the mood to go to a particular party, the host would often slip him a few shekels to come and help entertain his guests. Since his only other source of income was from begging, he was usually happy to oblige. He called it his "night job."

But deep inside Tuffy there was a lot of pain mixed in with the humor. He knew that many of the people who laughed at his jokes despised him. You see, people in those days had the idea that every illness or handicap was the direct result of a specific sin. So when a child was born blind, they believed that either his parents had done something terrible or God was punishing him in advance for sins that he would commit later. Even if he had done nothing wrong, he was still tainted by "bad blood" and, therefore, was not worthy of respect.

One day Tuffy was occupied in his "day job," begging near one of the entrances to the temple. He approached a rabbi and his group of students who were passing nearby.

"What's up, my friend?" the rabbi asked kindly.

"Duh!" Tuffy replied. "No offense, but isn't it a little obvious? I was born blind. Have you ever seen a blind carpenter? Have you ever seen a blind sea captain? Have you ever seen a rabbi who was born blind? I mean, they haven't even invented Braille yet, so how am I supposed to get a job? Can you help me out here?"

The rabbi was chuckling quietly, "I like this guy," he said to his students.

Then Tuffy heard those familiar but painful words. "Rabbi," one of the students asked, "Who sinned, this man or his parents, that he was born blind?"

The rabbi responded, "Wrong question. This blindness has nothing to do with this man's behavior or that of his parents. He is blind so that the work of God can be clearly seen in his life. Remember, I am the Light of the world."

I think I like this guy, thought Tuffy.

He recoiled at what happened next. He heard the rabbi spit on the ground. He had heard lots of people spit on the ground when they first met him. That was a way some showed their disgust for people they despised. Did this kind teacher say nice things and then act spitefully? He sensed the rabbi bending over, and then he heard the sound of activity on the ground at his feet. The Rabbi seemed to be mixing something. Then he straightened up. Suddenly Tuffy felt a slimy mess being spread over his eyes.

"Hey, what do you think you're doing?" yelled Tuffy, "That stuff is gross! Are you out of your mind?"

"It will be all right," said the rabbi. His voice still sounded kind. "Just go down to the Pool of Siloam and wash it off."

"Thanks a lot! By the time I get back I'll have lost ten shekels in income!" Grumpily he set off toward the Pool of Siloam, half a mile away. Behind him he could hear expressions of disgust from the students, but the rabbi was still chuckling, as if he knew something no one else knew.

Tuffy was puzzled. The smearing of his eyes had angered him, yet the rabbi seemed so kind and understanding. And he remembered the part about, "He is blind so that the work of God can be clearly seen in his life." Was something special about to happen to him? And what was this about the light of the world? Things just weren't adding up. *Oh well,* he thought. *First things first. Got to get this disgusting stuff off my face.*

He reached the pool a half hour later. He bent down and began to wash his face, scrubbing the skin over his eyes vigorously. Suddenly he saw a flash of . . . what? He saw something clear and liquid, and something else seemed to be in it. What was it? Could this be a reflection of *his* face? Suddenly it hit him, "I can see," he shouted. Then he froze. *Light of the world,* he thought. *So that's what this was all about!*

This amusing story functions as an acted parable in the Gospel of John. By healing the blind man, Jesus illustrated the truth of His earlier statement "I am the light of the world." As the Light of the world, Jesus brought physical sight to a man who was born blind. But this story holds a deeper meaning. It actually begins all the way back in chapter 7.

The Feast of Tabernacles

Chapters 7-10 of the Fourth Gospel are all set at the time of year when the Jews celebrated the Feast of Tabernacles, which commemorated the Exodus and the time of Israel's wandering in the wilderness (Lev. 23:43). During that wandering God provided Israel with water and light (Exod. 13:21-22; 17:1-7). So, two major themes of the feast were *water* (a water ceremony was a major feature of each day's festivities) and *light* (torchlight processions at night). People lived outside the city in shelters made from palm branches, reminding them of God's watch care in the wilderness. Tabernacles was the most popular of all the Jewish feasts. This reminder of the Exodus taught them that just as God provided water and food to Israel in the wilderness, so He can continue to provide the same for the needs of the present.

In Palestine there are two basic seasons of the year: an extremely dry summer of four to five months (virtually never rains) and a rainy season of equal length spanning the winter. The Feast of Tabernacles comes at the time of year when the summer drought ends (September/October). It also marked the planting of the winter grains and the harvest of fruit. If rain should fall during the feast, the people took it as a sign of God's blessing.

The "I AM" Texts in the Gospel of John

Chapters 7 and 8 of John's Gospel record a series of debates between Jesus and various elements of the crowd at the temple during the Feast of Tabernacles. The entire debate sequence seems repetitive and makes no progress at all. Jesus and His opponents agree on nothing even after long discussion. The reality is that it is not always possible for people to come to agreement in a sinful world. Even a person as perfect and wise as Jesus couldn't convince His opponents of who He was or of the truthfulness of His teachings. With the attitudes and mind-sets some people have, they can never be convinced—they will always come up with excuses not to change their thinking. Such are best left to themselves, as Jesus finally did.

Chapter 8 concludes with the dramatic statement of Jesus, "I tell you the truth, before Abraham was born, I am!" (8:58). This concluding assertion points to one of the major features of John 7 and 8, the presence of a number of special "I AM" statements (from the unusual Greek expression "*ego eimi,*" pronounced "aygo aymee") that Jesus made. What is clear from John 8 alone is that the "I AM" statements are of vital importance (8:24), that they are associated somehow with Jesus (8:28), and that they indicate that Jesus was in existence long before He came to this earth as a human being (8:58). Before we can fully grasp the meaning of the "I AM" statements in John 8, we need to survey their use throughout the Gospel.

Human Self-Identification. In two settings of the Gospel, Jesus uses the phrase *I am* in a purely human and ordinary way (4:26; 6:20). In these cases He identifies Himself to the Samaritan woman and to His disciples at a human level. Here, His use of *I am* is something like, "Hey, guys, it's me!" In these texts there is no clear theological significance to the phrase.

Divine Self-Identification. However, John's Gospel contains a more significant group of usages. Seven times Jesus uses the special *I AM* phrase with predicates: "I AM the _____." Mohammed Ali offered a similar usage when he said, "I am *the greatest!*" In the Gospel of John Jesus says, "I am the bread of life" (6:35), "I am the light of the world" (8:12; 9:5), "I am the gate" (10:7), "I am the good shepherd" (10:11), "I am the resurrection and the life" (11:25, 26), "I am the way, the truth, and the life" (14:6), and "I am the true vine" (15:1). These powerful predicates illustrate ways in which the divinity of Jesus benefits those who are in relationship with Him.

Absolute Use. Scholars call the third type of "I AM" statement in the Gospel of John the "absolute use." Jesus sometimes uses *I AM* all by itself to assert His full equality with the God of the Old Testament. "I am telling you now before it happens, so that when it does happen you will believe that I am He" (13:19, NIV). In the New International Version, the translators have supplied the word *He* in "I am He." In John 13:19, as well as John 8:24, 28, 58, Jesus is claiming the full qualities of the Godhead in language familiar from Old Testament references to Yahweh.

The "I AM" Texts in the Old Testament

Within the Old Testament, *I AM* functions as a name for God, expressing His continual availability to meet human need, His total uniqueness among all claimants to the title of "god," and His ability to foretell the future accurately. Prophets such as Ezekiel used the "I AM" expression in the context of the mighty works of salvation that the Lord will accomplish in the age to come. God will act as a Good Shepherd to feed and care for His people at the climax of earth's history.

Jesus declared that the future salvation that the prophets promised has become a present reality in Him. He *is* the Good Shepherd who was promised in Ezekiel 34 (see John 10:11). He *is* the divine Figure (John 8:24, 28, 58) who knows the future ahead of time (Isa. 46:9-10; John 13:19). Jesus is none other than the Yahweh of the Old Testament. He came down to shepherd His people just as He promised through the prophets (John 8:58). He is fully and truly God in the highest sense, even while walking on earth clothed in human flesh.

Because Jesus the man is also God, the future has become present in Christ. To those who believe in Him, He can deliver now the glories of the kingdom the Old Testament promised. In a real sense, we are already living in heavenly places in Christ Jesus (Eph. 2:6). Nothing is out of reach to those in relationship with Jesus. In Him the possibilities are limitless. The mighty things that God did occasionally in Old Testament times are brought to earth by Jesus and, through Him, by the Holy Spirit. He is the great I AM.

The Truth Sets You Free

While there are many things going on in John 7 and 8 that we do not have space to discuss here, I would like to reflect for a moment on the awesome comment of Jesus, "You will know the truth, and the truth will set you free" (John 8:32). How does the truth about Jesus set people free? I can think of at least four ways.

1. The truth brings freedom from fear. The disciple of Jesus never walks alone, no matter where he or she may go, and in the presence of Jesus, fear is gone, because "perfect love drives out fear" (1 John 4:18).

2. The truth brings freedom from self. For most people, the greatest handicap to a fulfilled life is found within themselves. Jesus has the power to change what we cannot change. We are no longer limited by our abilities and our natural motivations. In Christ, all things become new (2 Cor. 5:17; Rev. 21:5).

3. The truth also brings freedom from other people. Many people are paralyzed by fear of what other people may think of them. To know that we are acceptable to God means it no longer matters what other people think or say. We can think and act in terms of what is best instead of in terms of whether or not others will be pleased with us.

4. The truth brings freedom from sin. Many people have experienced the addictive power of sin. Sinners don't do what they like; they do what sin likes. Becoming Jesus' disciple breaks the chains of sin and empowers people to reach their full potential. "If the Son sets you free, you will be free indeed!" (John 8:36). The power of this statement is illustrated through an acted parable in chapter 9. Jesus heals a man born blind, freeing him in more ways than one.

The healing of the blind man creates a serious dilemma for the Pharisees (John 9:13-16). On the one hand, the healing points to the work of a man approved by God. But by performing a non-emergency healing on the Sabbath, Jesus appears to be acting like a false prophet (Deut. 13:1-5). The debate takes on a comical turn through the story's biting irony (9:17-34). The man who was blind sees more and more clearly that Jesus represents the true God of Israel. On the other hand, the Pharisees, who see clearly in the physical sense and who are supposed to be the guardians of the faith of Israel, become increasingly blind to the truth about Jesus (9:41).

So, Jesus' healing of the blind man becomes a symbol of His ability to bring spiritual insight, while the Pharisees' rejection of the healing symbolizes their rejection of the truth about God that Jesus revealed. The man finds the unbelief of the Pharisees amazing (9:30), especially since they admit that the miracle actually occurred (9:34). Their rejection is rooted in their willful blindness regarding the claims of Jesus.

Even today, few people reject Jesus because of a lack of evidence. Usually they reject Him because they don't want to let Him "tamper" with their lifestyle. It is easy to find excuses not to believe when we are protecting some cherished sin or attitude. The root reality of the unbeliever is unconfessed and unforsaken sin. These things "blind" one to the truths about Jesus.

Jesus Is the Good Shepherd

Verses 35-41 of chapter 9 set the stage for the Good Shepherd discourse of John 10. Jesus cares for the outcasts. When the leaders of a religious system excommunicate people because of their own enmity for Jesus, they demonstrate their blindness (9:39-41) and give Jesus the opportunity to collect these outcasts for Himself (John 9:35-38).

In ancient Palestine sheep pens were usually made from natural caves. The shepherd would lead the sheep into the cave in the evening and then lie down at the cave's entrance and sleep there. To reach the sheep, robbers or wild animals would have to physically get past the shepherd. Where caves were not available, farmers would build a fieldstone enclosure with an opening at one end just big enough for the shepherd to block with his body as he slept. So, when Jesus described Himself as the Good Shepherd and as the Gate for the sheep, listeners would have recognized that these concepts were two different ways of describing the same thing.

When Jesus describes Himself as the Gate through which the sheep must pass in order to be saved, He is delivering the same message as that found in Acts 4:12 ("Salvation is found in no one else") and John 14:6 ("I am the way and the truth and the life"). Jesus has replaced all other methods of salvation. There is no other way into the sheepfold than by the Gate. As the Gate of salvation, Jesus is the One who brings people to the Father. Eternal life is found in relationship with Jesus Christ (John 17:3).

As the Good Shepherd, Jesus is the One who takes care of those who have entered the sheep pen of the church. His two great qualifications for being the Good Shepherd are (1) that He is willing to lay down His life for the sheep (10:11-13, 17, 18) and (2) that He knows the sheep intimately (10:3, 14-16)—their welfare is His primary concern. Verse 21 clearly ties this part of the Gospel back to chapter 9. In John 10:1-21 Jesus is the Good Shepherd who heals the blind man and then rescues him from the spiritual abuse of the religious leaders. The blind man of John 9, in turn, was a sheep that recognized the voice of the Good Shepherd (John 10:4).

As the Good Shepherd, Jesus claimed for Himself those cast out by the religious leaders (9:34-38). The figure of speech in John 10, therefore, operates at two levels. In its original telling it was a rebuke to the religious leaders of John 9:40, who in their rough handling of the man born blind betrayed their true character as hired hands (10:12, 13). At the extended level of the Gospel itself, the story functioned to encourage the second generation, which faced treatment similar to that experienced by the man born blind. Jesus challenges the leaders of the church to care as much for the sheep as He does.

CHAPTER

A Devoted Soul and an Impending Cross

John 11:1–12:50

Emotions—can you trust them? Feelings—do they give a reliable picture of reality? They certainly seem to. I am what is known as a "night person." That means I'm wide awake in the evening but in another universe in the morning. If you call me at 5:30 in the morning, I'm likely to put the earpiece of the phone to my mouth and the mouthpiece to my ear and wonder why we have such a poor connection!

Along with this zombielike condition comes a feeling of deep depression. I'm no good to anybody, I'm a failure at all that I do, and nobody loves me. The amazing thing is that if I get up and get going, these feelings will pass in a few minutes. Were these depressed feelings a picture of reality? No, they're only the product of chemicals in the brain that follow a daily cycle. Feelings can be as fickle as the weather in Seattle. They can, nevertheless, be very convincing.

Mary of Bethany seems to be a good example of a highly emotional person. The Bible tells us that Mary was a "sinner" (Luke 7:37-39). While the woman of Luke 7 is not named, parallels with John 12, where Mary of Bethany anoints Jesus' feet, suggest that it is the same event and the same woman.* In this context, the term "sinner" implies sexual sin, perhaps prostitution. At some earlier point not recorded in the Bible, Mary came face to face with Jesus. I picture her falling down at His feet. Her feelings? Humiliation, guilt, self-hatred. But she sensed in Jesus a Man she could trust. He knew her in all her sinfulness, yet He loved her and accepted her. A healing process began.

On another occasion she is again at the feet of Jesus, this time basking in His presence (Luke 10:38-42). Martha is in the kitchen, and Mary is listening to Jesus. Here the emotions are upbeat. The scene is one of joy and contentment. Why? She had that "one thing that is needed," an intimate relationship with Jesus (Luke 10:42). Her feelings were under control and in tune with Jesus. Now that she had Jesus, she would never be depressed again, right? Wrong! One day her brother Lazarus got sick . . .

Looked at from the immediate perspective of Mary and Martha, the death of Lazarus was not the worst thing. The worst part about the situation was that Jesus had delayed His coming. How would you feel if your brother died because your doctor refused to come until the Super Bowl ended? Angry? Resentful? Depressed? All the above and more?

"Martha went out to meet him, *but* Mary stayed at home" (John 11:20, emphasis supplied). Perhaps Mary didn't *feel* like seeing Jesus just then. Fragile Mary was feeling hurt. The Man she had trusted seemed to have let her down. Why? Maybe He had rejected her. Maybe He was tired of her moods. Maybe their whole relationship had been a mistake!

---

* Ellen White supports this equation in *The Desire of Ages,* 557–568.

Had Christ been in the sickroom, Lazarus would not have died; for Satan would have had no power over him. . . . Therefore, Christ remained away. He suffered the enemy to exercise his power, that He might drive him back, a conquered foe. He permitted Lazarus to pass under the dominion of death; and the suffering sisters saw their brother laid in the grave. Christ knew that as they looked on the dead face of their brother their faith in their Redeemer would be severely tried. But He knew that because of the struggle through which they were now passing their faith would shine forth with far greater power.[1]

Relationships are such fragile things. Jesus is with Martha in the park just outside of town (11:17, 30); Mary stays in the house (11:20, 28-30). Both seem to be waiting for some kind of signal. This is a picture of our reality today. Jesus is always there, standing in the shadows of our life, waiting to be invited in. Sometimes, like Mary, our eyes are so blinded with tears that we can't see Him standing there with arms outstretched. Sometimes our ears are so deaf with anger, grief, or pain that we can't hear Him inviting us to come.

Only after Jesus sends Martha to invite Mary does she come out and once again fall at His feet (11:28-32). She repeats Martha's earlier complaint, but unlike Martha, she doesn't affirm continued faith in Him (11:32; cp. vs. 21, 22). As a result, she receives no revelation from Jesus, nor does He draw from her an expression of faith (cp. vs. 23-27). Instead, He seems deeply troubled at her lack of faith and that of those with her (v. 33; cp. v. 38). Jesus has come to invite them to behold the Resurrection and the Life, but their minds are fixed on their loss instead.

But Jesus speaks no words of rejection. Mary is back where she belongs, accepted at the feet of Jesus (v. 32). She is apparently still resentful, still insecure, still a raging sea of turbulent feelings. But Jesus doesn't walk away. He doesn't chide her for her feelings. He accepts her as she is. Her feelings do not in any way cause Him to change course.

Gaining Control Over Our Emotions

Why do our emotions have such a powerful effect on us? One very important reason is that by nature, human beings are absorbed in themselves. As important as it is to spend time in thoughtful reflection on our lives, there is a dark side to this concentration on one's own needs and feelings. This was brought home to me one day when I paid a visit to a mental hospital in New York City. The ward that I visited was filled with people in various stages of detachment from reality. But all the patients who could communicate revealed that they had one thing in common. Every last sentence was centered on the word *I*. Every conversation had one subject and only one. A self-centered person will always be a prisoner of his or her own emotions.

There is, however, a proven way to overcome self-centeredness and gain control of our feelings. Ellen White describes it: "It is a law of nature that our thoughts and feelings are encouraged and strengthened as we give them utterance."[2] Talk doubt and you will have more doubt. Talk discouragement and you will have more discouragement. But the reverse is also true. Talk faith and you will have more faith. Talk thankfulness and you will have joy. To quote Ellen White again from the same page: "Nothing tends more to promote health of body and of soul than does a spirit of gratitude and praise."

The ideal antidote to self-absorption and the depression that tends to come with it is a spirit of gratitude and praise. Words of thankfulness and praise take our minds off ourselves and direct them toward Jesus. Depression, of course, can result from chemical imbalances as well as self-defeating patterns of thinking. While "thank therapy" may even affect brain chemistry in many instances, medication is still required in others. And genuine sorrow in times of loss and on account of true guilt is certainly appropriate. Nevertheless, Ellen White's suggestion is a greatly underutilized strategy in the battle against runaway emotions.

While thankfulness and praise can make a huge difference in the way that we feel, no amount of thankfulness and praise, in themselves, could have brought Lazarus back from the dead. The only hope for one who had been dead four days was the life-giving power of Jesus. So, Jesus cried out in a loud voice, "Lazarus, come forth" (John 11:43, KJV).

The bottom line of Christian faith is that there is real power in the gospel. The power that raised Lazarus and Jesus from the dead is real, and it is still available today. There are times when only a miracle can clear away the clouds. We will all have the John 11 experience at one time or another. Death, betrayal, loss, and destruction may leave a real sense of loss that cannot be explained away. But at such points we can remember that the God who raised Jesus from the dead can still create something out of nothing. Even when all seems hopeless, we can still put our trust in Him.

Anointing for Burial

Mary stood in the shadows at the edge of the room, her heart once more filled with emotion as she contemplated this gathering of the most important people in her life. The others in the room were too busy enjoying the party to take notice of her quiet reverie.

There was Martha, bustling in and out of the room, preparing food, serving, and directing helpers with her usual efficiency. Good old Martha—a little uptight maybe, but you could always count

82

on her to be there when you needed somebody. And how she could cook! She had been real sweet since their brother Lazarus had been raised from the dead.

Oh yes, Lazarus. Mary's eyes moved to the center of the room, where Lazarus was reclining, a guest of honor along with Jesus. Mary never tired of gazing at the wonderful face of the dear brother she had given up for lost. Her eyes tenderly caressed his features, every curl of his beard, every movement of his mouth as he explained over and over what it felt like to be tied up like a mummy. Life was good!

Her eyes moved from Lazarus to Jesus. Wonderful, wonderful Jesus! Her face beamed with joy as she gazed on His animated face. While He told stories, His expression projected kindness. Was it possible to love anyone more than she loved Jesus? Mary's heart began to pound with excitement as she reached under her outer garment and felt the flask of expensive perfume, worth a whole year's wages. Jesus was worth any gift, any sacrifice. How could she ever have doubted Him? She remembered the look on His face when she had chided Him for not coming to Bethany sooner when Lazarus was ill. He wasn't so much hurt as disappointed. Well, she would never disappoint Him again!

Mary had heard disturbing rumors about plots to kill Jesus. Lazarus had even told her that Jesus believed that He would be killed on His next trip to Jerusalem. She wasn't much for flowers at funerals; she liked to do her giving while people were still alive to appreciate the gifts. She felt convinced that this was the time and place to demonstrate her devotion to Jesus. It might be her last chance. But in front of all these people?

Her gaze fell upon Simon, the host, and she wavered. Simon was the head elder at the synagogue. He, more than anyone else, knew all about her sinful past. And she and Simon knew something no one else knew. He had been the first. He was the one who had cast a long glance at her over the potluck table years before. He was the one who used his spiritual stature to charm and overwhelm a vulnerable young woman. He was the one who started her down the road to destruction from which Jesus eventually saved her.

For some reason, though, she never felt angry at Simon. As she gazed into his face just then, she felt no anger, only shame. He was a good man, the leader of the synagogue. Surely it was somehow her fault that he had transgressed with her. That's why she had never exposed him—she blamed herself. Her heart filled with shame once more. What if everyone laughed when she anointed Jesus? What if Simon called the police, as he had the time . . .? She shuddered and moved deeper into the shadows, seeking a way to sneak unseen out of the room and head home for a good cry.

But wait. Hadn't she confessed her sins to Jesus (being careful not to name Simon)? Hadn't He accepted her? If Jesus accepted her, did it really matter what anyone else thought? Hadn't He told her how valuable she was to God? Her courage began to rise as she remembered all the affirmations Jesus had given her, as she recalled the amazing changes He had brought into her life. She loved Him with every fiber of her being. She would do anything, go anywhere for Him. She would die for Him if need be. Why should she hesitate now just because Simon was there?

Her thoughts turned once more to the rumors about Jesus' impending death. Her jaw set with determination. Drawing the precious flask of perfume from beneath her outer garment, she began to move decisively toward the center of the room . . .

Mary Devotes Her Soul

The narrative at the beginning of John 12 deliberately contrasts Mary's wholehearted faith in and love for Jesus with the cold-hearted calculations of Caiaphas (at the end of chapter 11) and Judas (in the context of the story). In John's account of this event, Judas becomes the object of a subtle yet penetrating irony. He claims that the lavishing of perfume as an anointing for burial is a wasteful act (12:5). Yet by betraying Jesus, he becomes the one largely responsible for its necessity. Judas expresses concern for the poor. Yet in stealing from the purse, he makes it clear that the only poor person he cares about is himself (vs. 5, 6). Later on in the Gospel, the disciples think that Judas is leaving the upper room to give something to the poor when in fact he is going out to betray Jesus for a price (13:21, 26-30). Yet in another sense, no one ever gave more to the "poor" than Judas did when his betrayal sent Jesus to His death on the cross!

In the narrative Judas becomes the foil to Mary's devotion. Her anointing of Jesus' feet is motivated by unselfish love and sacrifice. Judas's criticism of Mary, on the other hand, is motivated by greed and deceit. Once again Jesus demonstrates that He knows what is in the heart of another person, but He does not expose Judas's motivations to public view. Instead, He defends Mary by pointing out that social action (helping the poor), as important as that may be, is ultimately meaningless apart from the Cross (12:7, 8). Honoring Jesus is far more valuable than money, but Judas will soon accept thirty pieces of silver to dishonor Him.

In this scene we see Mary's total devotion. She trembles with gratitude to the One who saved her brother and who is about to die for her. The perfume she pours on Jesus cost her a year of hard work (possibly humiliating, shameful work such as prostitution). But it represented her whole life, gratefully offered to Jesus. Such total devotion is rarely popular, as Judas's reaction makes clear. "What a waste," people say. "You could have done great things with your life, but you chose to waste it on Jesus!"

Judas's reaction is normal and human. Mary's action does seem a waste. What church board would approve such an expenditure? To human reasoning, Mary seems emotionally disturbed. A devoted soul makes us uncomfortable. But notice again how Jesus felt about it, this time as recorded in Mark 14:6-9: "She has done a beautiful thing to me. . . . She did what she could. . . . I tell you the truth, wherever the gospel is preached throughout the world, what she has done will also be told, in memory of her."

The world owes Mary a debt. She was the only human being who comforted Jesus on the way to the cross. In this verse we see how Jesus treasures the devoted soul. How many times I wish I could have comforted Him. How gladly I would have wiped His brow, carried His cross, spoken an encouraging word. If only I . . . Well, she did! And it meant a lot to Jesus.

Can we comfort Jesus today? Hebrews tells us that it is possible for human beings to crucify the Son of God afresh (Heb. 6:4-6). If that is true, then we can also comfort Him afresh! We can comfort Him in the wholehearted devotion of all our feelings to Him. When we love Him, praise Him, cherish Him, it makes a difference to Him!

How can you and I become devoted like Mary? First, such devotion comes only in response to the devotion of Another. We love Him because He first loved us. We forgive others because we have been forgiven. It was the cross of Jesus that became the focus of Mary's emotions. Her understanding of what Jesus had done for her, the value that she had in His eyes, called every fiber of her being to respond in kind.

Second, as we learn that expression deepens impression, we will spend more time expressing faith and less time expressing doubt; more time expressing thankfulness and less time expressing disappointment; more time expressing encouragement and less time expressing condemnation. As we train ourselves to obey Jesus in our conscious expressions, our emotions and our reactions will more and more reflect devotion to Him.

Finally, we must pray for total devotion to Jesus. Even the best of us find ourselves divided in our affections. Take hold of that small part of you that desires to be fully devoted to the Lord. Encourage that desire, pray about it, offer it to God (see Rom. 6:11-14 for a clear and practical expression of this principle) and that part of you will grow stronger and stronger until it becomes the dominating attitude of your life. Let me illustrate this from my own experience.

I was a single pastor in New York City. One day a beautiful girl entered my congregation. She had come from North Dakota to New York City to get away from her problems. As a conscientious pastor, of course, I arranged to study the Bible with her three or four times a week! It was not long before my plans for her went far beyond her baptism. As our relationship grew, however, it was clear that there was a problem. She could not stand the city that I loved. Her heart longed for the flat, treeless plains of her home state.

A short time after her baptism, word came that her great-grandfather had died. She and her mother borrowed money to purchase *one-way* tickets to the funeral. At the airport I had the distinct impression that she didn't plan to return. I feebly offered to pay their trip back. Then the plane was gone, and I went out into darkness of soul. For days I was angry with God. "Why did You tease me like this and then take her away?" On my knees I begged God to bring her back to me even if it wasn't His will. In essence, I prayed, "Not Your will but mine be done, O Lord." I was a turbulent sea of seething emotions.

In the midst of my darkness a still, small voice said, "If it's not God's will, such a marriage will never work."

"I don't care; I want her," I replied. But gradually, 20 percent of me learned to pray that God's will be done while 80 percent wanted her at any cost. Amazingly, as I continued to pray, God's will became increasingly important to me. A few days later it seemed that 40 percent of me wanted God's will and 60 percent wanted mine.

Shortly after that I was on my knees at 11 P.M., pleading with God for a new heart. Suddenly it happened. I knew that I wanted God's will more than anything. I prayed, "Thank You, Lord, for changing me. Do Your will, whatever it is. If she never comes back, I will praise Your name anyway. No matter what, Lord, do Your will with me." A tremendous sense of peace and assurance came over me. My whole soul was dedicated to Him. As I said Amen— I'm not exaggerating a bit here—at the very instant "Amen" passed through my mind, the phone rang. It was a collect call from Pam. She wanted to know if I was still interested in sending her some plane tickets! That was more than thirty years ago. She has been my treasure and my joy ever since.

God is often willing to give us the desires of our hearts if we will only devote ourselves fully to Him, as Mary did. Although our feelings naturally range up and down, by His grace they can be increasingly devoted to Him. The God who transformed Mary still lives today and longs for our devotion. There is no greater joy than in response to such love.

---

1. *The Desire of Ages*, 528.
2. *The Ministry of Healing*, 251.

CHAPTER 10

Real Greatness

John 13:1-30; 17:1-26

It was an upstairs room. In the corner of the room there was a small table. On the table was a large pitcher full of water, a basin, and a towel. One thing was missing: There was no servant to wash the group's feet. The disciples all hung around acting as if there was nothing for them to do.

"Nice weather we've been having lately."

"Did you notice that the Tiberias Stock Exchange went down yesterday?"

"Yeah, that's the way things go sometimes."

Moments passed and nobody moved toward the table in the corner. The problem was not so much that the task required touching dirty feet. The problem was that washing feet was a slave's job. Washing feet was for nobodies, for people who didn't aspire to greatness. The disciples all planned to be great. After all, wasn't that why they were with Jesus? Soon He would proclaim Himself king, drive out the Romans, and one of them would be top dog, right next to Him. Whoever took up the towel and the basin would take himself right out of the running for that position. Better to sit around with dirty feet than to admit that you were a nobody!

> Each of the disciples, yielding to wounded pride, deter-
> mined not to act the part of the servant. . . . How could
> [Jesus] show that it is loving service, true humility, which
> constitutes real greatness? . . . He had full consciousness of
> His divinity, but He . . . laid aside His royal crown and
> kingly robes, and [took] the form of a servant.[1]

What is real greatness? Real greatness is the King of the universe walking over to the corner of a room, picking up a towel and a basin of water, and stooping down to wash the feet of an unstable disciple like Peter and a traitor like Judas. Real greatness doesn't need to brag or assert itself. Real greatness exercises self-control and can act the role of a slave. Real greatness does what needs to be done despite everyone else's derision and scorn.

Real greatness means having the same attitude as Jesus, who was "in very nature God" yet "taking the very nature of a servant" He "humbled himself" (Phil. 2:5-8). Real greatness means considering "others better than yourself" (Phil 2:3). Real greatness means following Jesus in the path of service and humility. Or as Jesus Himself put it, "Whoever serves me must follow me; and where I am, my servant also will be" (John 12:26).

If you and I had been in the upper room that night, would we have acted differently from the disciples? If our first thought in any situation is of our self-interest, we are pursuing a false greatness. If our first reaction to any situation is to nag, belittle, criticize, and complain, we are exhibiting the opposite of humility.

Putting other people down says, "I am better than you." On the other hand, considering others better than yourself causes you to uplift, encourage, and praise them. In basketball or hockey, the truly great players are not the ones who score the most points, but those who make all the players around them better.

How can we develop real greatness? How can we learn to love a life of service? Not by trying to be humble. That usually only makes things worse. The key to developing an attitude like Christ's is to focus on Him (Phil. 2:5). When we feed on Christ (John 6), when we focus on His words (John 6:63) and His example (John 13:12-17), we become molded more and more into His image (2 Cor. 3:18). By beholding we become changed.

The Other Path to Greatness

In the book *The Desire of Ages* Ellen White examines the feelings and motives of Judas as the time of Jesus' crucifixion approached.[2] She wrote:

> The prospect of having a high place in the new kingdom had led Judas to espouse the cause of Christ. . . .[He] was continually advancing the idea that Christ would reign as king in Jerusalem. . . . It was he who set on foot the project to take Christ by force and make Him king. . . . [He hoped to secure] the first position, next to Christ, in the new kingdom.

Judas chose to follow a different path to greatness from that exhibited by Christ in the foot-washing service. On this particular point he considered himself wiser than Christ. Surely it was obvious to everyone that greatness came from power, wealth, and the esteem of others! But Judas's logical course of action led only to his destruction.

He failed to realize that anyone can act great or demand to be treated as great. Given the opportunity, anyone can spend money or command others. It takes *real* greatness to act the part of a servant and do tasks that others should have done. It takes real greatness to put others first, to treat others as better than oneself.

When Jesus Prayed for You

Before the first Gulf War began, a team of three U.S. Special Forces soldiers were airlifted 160 miles into Iraq at night to gather intelligence. As morning approached they dug a foxhole, got into it and covered it with greenery as camouflage. There they were going to sit out the day, get out at night, and then head home.

Well, it wasn't long into that morning before one of the soldiers began to wonder what was going on around them. He lifted the camouflage just a little bit and found himself face to face with an Iraqi girl about seven years old. He knew instantly that if he pulled her into the foxhole, she would scream; so the only way to preserve the mission was to kill her on the spot and pull the body into the foxhole. But he found himself unable to do that. So he tried to tell her in sign language not to tell her father or anybody else, and he let her go. But tell her father is exactly what she did. Almost at once the foxhole was surrounded by several hundred Iraqi soldiers. The bullets were flying, and heavier equipment was on its way.

The U.S. soldiers radioed back to Saudi Arabia and said, "We need help. We need help *now!*" A Black Hawk helicopter was sent out immediately. It flew the 160 miles in less than one hour, flying low to the ground so as to avoid radar. In fact, the Black Hawk flew so low the pilot had to perform an incredible gyration to avoid a camel making its way across the desert! The helicopter arrived on the scene, circled the foxhole a few times spraying ammunition in all directions, and then landed. The three men jumped in and had a wild Disney ride all the way back to Saudi Arabia. No one was hurt.

This story illustrates the incredible power of "command and control" military communication. The difference between the allied coalition and Iraq during the first Gulf War was the ability to communicate when the time was right.

When I heard this story, I remember asking myself, "Is there a spiritual lesson here?" I believe there is. In the New Testament, Christian life is often described in terms of warfare. What is the "command and control" of Christian warfare? What is the key to success in the battle of Armageddon (Rev. 16:14-16), the last great battle of earth's history? According to the Bible, that battle will not be a military conflict so much as a spiritual one (see verse 15). Spiritual warfare does not have to do with AK-47 rifles, M1A1 tanks, and F-15 fighter-bombers. Spiritual warfare has to do with demolishing "arguments and every pretension that sets itself up against the knowledge of God," and taking "captive every thought to make it obedient to Christ" (2 Cor. 10:5).

Christian warfare is a battle for the mind. So I asked myself the questions: If Christian life is a battle for the mind, if warfare is an appropriate metaphor for Christian living, then what can we learn from the Gulf War about the Christian life? What is the crucial element that makes the difference between victory and defeat? I believe John 17 has the answers.

To close His farewell gathering with His disciples (John 13-17), Jesus prayed an intercessory prayer that has three parts. First He prayed for Himself (17:1-5). Then He turned His attention to His disciples and their need for support in His physical absence (vs. 6-19). Finally, He began to pray in behalf of the second generation—those who would come to faith through the word of the disciples rather than the direct ministry of Jesus (v. 20 and on).

What is interesting here is that Jesus prayed for others even though He said that others should pray to Him (14:14). Prayer is not simply a means of communication between creatures and the Creator; it is embedded in the very communication system of the Godhead (14:16)!

Above all else, the focus of Jesus' prayer for the later generations of His people was unity, a unity fashioned after the unity between Jesus and the Father (17:21, 22). So, intercessory prayer is like a web of communication that has always existed among the members of the Godhead; it ties all who are in relationship with God into a giant network. It is as essential to the accomplishment of God's work on earth as command and control was in the Gulf War.

Despite all the power that Jesus displayed in the course of His ministry on earth, He still saw great value in praying for others. Somehow prayer for others accomplishes things that would never happen otherwise.

The Power and the Peril of Prayer for Others

I've learned three things about this kind of prayer. First, it works. Second, it's dangerous. Third, it's good for us.

1. Intercessory prayer works. Once while I was visiting in Australia, a pastor and his wife asked for healing. I said, "That's something I don't feel particularly gifted for, but if you really want to try, I'm willing. If you don't mind, I'd like to have the conference president with us because he's a man of God and of prayer."

We went into a back room at the church. Roland Hegstad was the other speaker for that service, so I said to him, "You preach while we pray in the back. Then I'll come out and do my part."

When I came out and sat on the platform, he leaned over during a song and asked, "What was going on in the back room?"

"What do you mean?"

"I have never in my life felt such a sense of the Lord's power in my preaching as during the past hour. It felt like 'radiation' coming out of the back room."

I discovered later that this unusual burst of energy wasn't so much a result of my prayers—back in the U.S., my wife was praying for me at exactly the same time. I have come to the place where I can often sense when my wife is praying for me even when I'm on the other side of the world. (To finish the story: I met the pastor and his wife six years later, and she had no further trace of the potentially fatal illness about which we had prayed.)

In the church I attend, which has about 150 members, we take time to share and pray together each Sabbath. Without telling anyone, a friend of mine began taking notes on our prayers. One Sabbath he got up and said, "Do you people have any idea what's going on in this church when we pray? I've been keeping track for over a year, and God has granted us 80 percent of what we've prayed for this year! Clinically speaking [he's a psychologist!], this is overwhelming evidence: Prayer makes a difference." Intercessory prayer works.

God already knows our problems before we ask, so why should intercessory prayer make a difference? I don't know why, but I do know that it works. I am reminded of Daniel, which tells us that Daniel's prayers turned a whole nation around. I don't know why that happened, but I know it did. Prayer for others makes a difference.

2. Intercessory prayer is dangerous. During the war in Vietnam, the U.S. forces commonly sent out squads of about 12 heavily armed men and a 13th man who was unarmed or lightly armed. This 13th man wasn't a medic; he was the radio man, with heavy equipment to carry on his back.

Which man did the Viet Cong shoot at first? The ones with the heaviest weapons? No, they always went for the radio man. Why? Because the radio man was the key: With a simple call, he could change the battle odds. He could call in an air strike or an artillery barrage. He could turn twelve men into twelve thousand on short notice. The radio man could bring the decisive numbers to the decisive point.

The radio man could also act as intelligence. He could detect enemy signals. He knew where the enemy was, how strong they were, what kind of attack was coming, and could radio that information back to headquarters. In Vietnam, the radio man was the key to the battle and the Viet Cong knew that. So it was dangerous to carry the radio.

The Christian "command and control" element is intercessory prayer. Because of the power of this kind of prayer, Satan often attacks—in a variety of ways—those who pray. He'll do anything to keep God's people from praying. He'll keep us busy with other things. If that doesn't work, he'll seek to threaten and harm. But even though people who pray for others place themselves in the danger zone, the benefits of such prayer far outweigh any dangers.

3. Intercessory prayer is good for us. Praying for people we don't like changes our attitude toward them. It is hard to pray for someone and retain a strong dislike for that person. When we pray for people we don't naturally like, we become more like Jesus, who prayed even for His enemies. Since Jesus prayed for us (John 17), we should certainly pray for one another.

When we pray for other people, we ourselves often receive in kind. When we pray that someone will come to Christ and be forgiven, we often receive the assurance that our own sins are forgiven. When we pray for people who have hurt us, we experience forgiveness for the times we have hurt others. As we pray for others, we ourselves are blessed. And in the process we share the Lord's concerns for other people and thereby develop a deeper relationship with the Lord.

And perhaps most important, prayer for others can give us a great sense of fulfillment as we realize we are making a difference in the world. There is nothing more fulfilling than to know that the world is a better place because we were here, and prayer for others is perhaps the *most* powerful way to make a difference.

The "How To" of Praying for Others

If you are like me, prayer for others has been somewhat of an up-and-down experience. Is there any way to change ingrained habits of making prayer the last and least part of our day? Here are a few practical suggestions.

First of all, it helps to have a regular time set aside for prayer—if possible, the same time every day. That helps to build a habit.

Second, make a list. Yes, I know—you've tried that before. But sometimes I think we can make a prayer list too long. We can have a list of people to pray for that is so long that we never get through it, and after a while it just seems like more work than it is worth.

May I suggest a short list? At the top of the list put the most hopeless person you know. Who is that? You know who I mean! It's the person who, no matter what you do, remains abusive, hopeless, and impossible. Nothing you've ever tried seems to help. Put the person who bugs you the most at the top of the list so you can learn the experience of praying for difficult people. (No doubt you're on the top of somebody else's list—or should be!) An amazing thing happens when you pray for somebody who causes you trouble: Your feelings toward that person begin to change. You begin to see possibilities in that person.

Along with that more difficult person, let me suggest that you put a few more promising types on your list so you can see results right away, because results are encouraging. Keep the list rather short, and as the Lord moves you, take someone off the list and add another.

Third, most of us accomplish very little in life without some kind of accountability. We all can use a "hard-nosed" friend—someone to hold us accountable to our promises and resolutions. I define a hard-nosed friend as a person who's willing to challenge me to be all that I can be. Let's say you tell your friend that you're going to spend from 7:00 - 7:15 A.M. daily in intercessory prayer. You invite him or her to hold you accountable. The next morning at 7:17 the phone rings. It's your friend, who says, "Did you?" A hard-nosed friend is the kind of friend who will tell you to your face what you need to hear even when you don't really want to hear it.

Intercessory prayer is the key to victory in Christian warfare. Perhaps God is calling you to be a key player in His "command and control" team.

At the fringes of John 13–17 we discover the essence of true greatness, a turning away from self to service for others. That kind of service includes both everyday tasks such as washing feet (13:1-17) and deeply spiritual service such as intercessory prayer (17:6-26). The exciting truth of the Fourth Gospel is that Jesus is the greatest revelation of what God is like. And the God He reveals does not live to be served, but to serve (see Matt. 20:28; Mark 10:45)! And He calls us to treat others the way He has treated us (John 13:15).

1. *The Desire of Ages*, 644, 645.
2. See ibid., 718–721.

CHAPTER 11

The Spirit Replaces Jesus

John 13:31–16:33

After Jesus washed the feet of all the disciples, the shadow of the cross began to intrude into the room where they were reclining. The disciples began to realize that Jesus was truly about to leave them. John 13–16 records what Jesus told His disciples about how to live without His physical presence. What He said would be just as helpful to the second generation of Christians, who would have to live without the physical presence of the disciples.

While world-class sound bites fill this section of the Gospel of John, the flow of the material can be difficult to follow. It's almost as if John tossed the great sayings of Jesus into a basket and then put them into his Gospel in whatever order he happened to pull them out. No doubt Jesus' discourse was much longer than what John recorded for us. He decided to preserve all he could of Jesus' instruction, even if the flow is difficult to follow.

Such Sweet Sorrow?

"It'll be better for you if I go away," said Jesus (John 16:7). Or as the New International Version puts it, "It is for your good that I am going away." The disciples must have had a hard time believing this. It is tough to see any good in the loss of someone you love. How can it be for your good when a very vital piece of you has been torn away and put out of reach? "Parting is such sweet sorrow," said Shakespeare. I know about the sorrow. I'm not so sure about the sweet.

She and I had a bitter-sweet relationship a long time ago. At its best it had been very good. We had a lot of things in common. Our differences often balanced each other out. We talked easily and at great length. Our standards and tastes were similar. But there had been many hard times as well. She was easygoing, but I was not mature enough to let her be herself. I tried hard to make her over into my image of the ideal woman. She tried hard to comply. But the more I succeeded in changing her, the less I liked what she became!

That summer we decided to break up but remain friends. It didn't work well. We couldn't stand being together and we couldn't stand being apart. So one day she came to me with a solution to the difficulties in our relationship.

"I've decided to go home. That way we can each start over again," she said. Home was a country three thousand miles away.

"No way," I responded. "I'll miss you too much. I'll go crazy without you. Let's keep trying; I'm sure we can work it out."

"I don't think so," she said. "We've been trying for two years. It's just not working."

"Aw, come on," I said. "Just one more chance. If you go away, my life will be ruined."

"No, it won't," she replied. "It'll be better for you if I go away."

I wasn't convinced.

A week later we stood in silence at the airport terminal gate. There was nothing left to say. All the talking, all the crying, had left us exhausted and empty. She handed the flight attendant her boarding pass and entered the jetway. As I watched her disappear out of sight, her words kept ringing in my ears: "It'll be better for you if I go away."

I never saw her again.

Genuine Love

Jesus is going away, and the disciples feel abandoned. How can they possibly continue without Him? But Jesus makes it clear that His going away to the Father will benefit them (John 16:7). His presence with the Father will empower their love (13:34, 35), their prayers (14:13, 14), and their obedience (14:15, 21) through the Holy Spirit whom He will send (14:16, 17).

Human love tends to focus on objects of attraction or on those who have something to offer us in return. It focuses on the beautiful, the rich, the impressive, the powerful. But the love of Jesus' disciples was to be of a different nature. They were to love one another the way Jesus had loved them (13:34, 35). People don't normally help when it isn't convenient, give when it hurts, or face ridicule and accusations without fighting back. When the disciples loved as Jesus loved, people would know that something special had taken place.

How does one learn to love like that? The ways we express love to other people are the ways we ourselves have experienced love. When the "love" we have received is abusive and controlling, we tend to "love" others in abusive and controlling ways. We can learn to truly love others only to the extent that we have allowed ourselves to experience Jesus' love. Those who are much loved can love much.

In Jesus' farewell talk in John 13–16, He pointed to His relationship with the Father as the model for the disciples' relationship with Himself. Jesus loves the disciples the way the Father loves Him (15:9). The disciples are to obey His commands just as He obeys His Father's commands (15:10). Similarly, the relationship of unbelievers to the disciples will parallel the world's relationship to Jesus (15:18). The world's hatred of the disciples grows out of its hatred of Jesus (15:22-25). The values of the world are often the opposite of God's values. So, in a world that does not lightly tolerate threats to its control, the disciple of Jesus will often feel out of place.

But for the disciples, the negative experience of hatred and persecution (15:18-25; 16:1-4) is counterbalanced by the benefits that will come to them because Jesus has gone to the Father and has sent His Spirit into the world (15:26, 27; 16:7-15).

Jesus Says Goodbye

Though He's saying goodbye, Jesus wants His disciples to know that His going away will not end His ministry. Two substitutes will replace Jesus' personal, physical presence. Jesus will continue to manifest Himself and His Father to them through the Holy Spirit. But that is not all. As branches connected to the Vine by the Spirit, the disciples themselves will take Jesus' place in the world. Through their words and their writings, they will make Jesus real to a new generation. What is particularly exciting about this concept is that in today's world the words and actions of believers can be the clearest—and are often the only—picture of Jesus that many people will ever see.

Why was it for the disciples' good that Jesus was going away? Jesus suggests a number of reasons, two of which I have just mentioned: (1) Jesus will send the Holy Spirit, who will not be subject to the human limitations that Jesus was subject to. Through the Spirit, all the benefits of Jesus' ministry will continue to be theirs. (See John 14:16, 17; 14:26, 27; 15:26, 27; 16:7-15. I'll say more about these texts later.) (2) Through the efforts of the disciples under the influence of the Spirit, the work of Jesus would be spread throughout the world and would impact every people and place (14:12).

In addition, Jesus' intercessory presence with the Father would empower the disciples' prayers to new heights (14:13, 14). The work of the Holy Spirit would make Jesus' love real in their lives, which would have convincing power in the world (15:12-15; 13:34, 35). Their deeper love for Jesus and one another would empower their obedience to Jesus' commands (14:15, 21). This heightened level of obedience would bring great joy even in the midst of their sorrow over Jesus' departure (15:10, 11; 16:20-22). And their experience in coping with Jesus' absence would enable them to provide a solid foundation for the second generation. Like branches on a vine, they would bring forth much fruit (15:1-8).

Although it must have been difficult for the disciples to accept Jesus' statement that He was going away for their good, time and experience have proven it to be true. So it was when the young woman went home to make her life and mine better. She is happily married and has been very successful in her career, and I too have been richly blessed since the time she left. She was not to blame for the difficulties in our relationship, yet her selfless act ended up benefiting us both. Perhaps Shakespeare had it right after all when he wrote "parting is such sweet sorrow."

A Replacement

Buster was a fairly ordinary cat, but we loved him. He was no breed in particular, and his coloring was strange in a very ordinary way (tabby), but he was a delightful combination of the two characteristics that make cats so much fun. On the one hand, he was all cat. The mice, chipmunks, squirrels, moles, and birds in the area were all intensely aware of his presence whenever he ventured outside. The "mighty hunter" strode through his domain (ours and the neighboring yards) with an air of conscious superiority. His cat-play antics kept my kids amused for hours at a time. On the other hand, when he was with children, he was as gentle and affectionate as if there were not a violent chromosome in his whole genetic makeup. He was greatly loved.

Buster was never absent from our house for more than twelve hours (except for the couple of times he showed up at Grandma's house a mile away—following up memories of an early childhood "cat-sitting" experience, I suppose). Then one day he disappeared. There was no trace of him for seventy-two hours. Our worries and fears increased by the hour after the first day or so. After three days the family gathered for a special prayer session. I can still hear my wife praying, "Lord, even if he is dying somewhere, please bring him back so we can know what happened. Send Your angel to carry him back if You have to. We need to know what has happened to him."

My wife's prayers have always been dangerously effective. The next morning she was having devotions by the front window when she suddenly screamed out, "It's Buster! It's Buster! He's back! He's in the yard!" We all piled out of the house in various stages of dress and undress to greet the beloved wanderer. He lay at the farthest corner of the yard, obviously completely exhausted. There was a large hole in his side, filled with flies and maggots. With both tears and joy we realized that my wife's prayers had been answered. Buster had come home to say goodbye!

With broken hearts we gently carried him back into the house and called the vet. But although there was an initial burst of recovery under medication, he had a massive relapse, and the family went to the animal hospital to say a final goodbye to our brave little sweetheart. When he saw us, he struggled catfully to his feet to greet us and then collapsed back to the floor of his cage, barely able to breathe or open his eyes. We knew that it was over. With loud wailing and two buckets of tears the five of us expressed our love to him one last time. We walked out of the animal hospital into sunshine, but the day seemed so dark.

When the news of Buster's death came, my wife turned immediately to the kids. "I know what we need to do. You deserve to have the joy and affection of an animal. We need to go straight to the pet store and find a replacement for Buster."

Our teen said, "No way! No cat could ever replace Buster!"

But my wife was not deterred from her purpose. A few hours later, Snooper (the nosiest cat you ever saw) was exploring the house. He was as lacking in breeding as Buster. He had tortoise-shell markings and extra soft fur. He was just as gentle and much more disobedient (why should the humans have sole use of tabletops, counters, and cupboards?). Did he replace Buster? Yes and no. When you lose someone you love, something is always lost that can never be replaced. But in other ways Snooper is just as special as Buster was. He fills a unique place in our hearts. (One thing would make our situation complete: to have both of them with us all the time. Maybe when Jesus comes back . . .)

Introducing the Spirit

Eleven passages in the Gospel of John refer either directly or indirectly to the nature and work of the Holy Spirit. Five of these passages are scattered throughout the first half of the book. Another occurs in relation to an appearance of Jesus after His resurrection (20:22). The other five passages are part of the farewell discourse in John 13–16.

The five early passages mention the Spirit only in passing, offering little information about the exact nature of His work. It is as if John was using these passages to plant seeds in the reader's mind that would sprout only in the fertile soil of Jesus' farewell speech. From these early passages we learn that the Spirit makes it possible for the Baptist to identify Jesus at the Jordan (1:32, 33). He is an essential part of human participation in the kingdom of God (3:5, 6). Worship is no longer tied to specific locations or temples, nor is it limited to any particular people (4:23, 24). The Spirit is available in every place and to anyone of any background through the words of Jesus (6:63). We can see the exact nature of the Spirit's work only in the context of the Cross (7:39). The passage at the end of the Gospel tells us that Jesus "breathed on them and said, 'Receive the Holy Spirit' (20:22). This passage shows that the promise of John 7:39 began to be fulfilled right after Jesus' "glorification" on the Cross.

As we have mentioned, five crucial passages about the Holy Spirit are clustered at the heart of Jesus' farewell discourse (John 14:16, 17; 14:26; 15:26; 16:7-11; 16:13-15). John tells us that Jesus gave the Holy Spirit an unusual name. He used a Greek noun that has sometimes been transliterated into English as "Paraclete." This term is usually translated as "Comforter" or "Counselor."

Paraclete refers to a person who is "called alongside to help" someone. So the word can be used in the legal sense of a defense attorney at a trial who appeals in behalf of someone else. The word *Counselor,* then, has a strong legal connotation that fits well with the Spirit's role as a witness who aids the disciples in their witness for Jesus (15:26).

However, the idea of the Spirit as a *Comforter* (called alongside to comfort) is not foreign to Jesus' farewell discourse either. The disciples would be bereft like orphans if the Spirit were not sent to them after Jesus' departure (14:18). The Spirit comes to help them cope with their grief at the loss of physical contact with Jesus (16:6, 7).

Jesus' purpose in sending the Holy Spirit is twofold. First, He "remains with them forever." In other words, He provides the disciples with a permanent divine presence. Second, since the Holy Spirit is called "another Counselor," Jesus was the original "Counselor" to the disciples. Jesus' designation of the Holy Spirit as "another Counselor" means that the Spirit has come to take Jesus' place during the time that He is in heaven and consequently absent from the disciples.

From our study of the Gospel of John it is clear that the work of the Spirit is very important. But interest in the Spirit is not healthy if it directs our attention away from Jesus. The Spirit has not come to draw attention to Himself; He comes to exalt and glorify Jesus in the estimation of humanity (16:13). The Spirit is Jesus' Representative, or Ambassador, here on earth. When we listen to the Spirit, we are listening to Jesus Himself (14:16, 17; 14:26; 15:26; 16:7-11; 16:13-15).

It is in this sense that the Holy Spirit can be said to replace Jesus. The Spirit is Christ's Successor and Representative both with the disciples and to the world (John 14:16, 17). The teaching that Jesus could no longer do in the flesh, the Spirit would do everywhere in His behalf (14:26; 16:13). The witness that He would no longer bear, the Spirit would bear in His behalf (15:26). Through the Spirit, Jesus would continue to be glorified on earth (16:14).

On the other hand, as Jesus brought judgment and conviction to all who were exposed to His light (3:18-21), so the Holy Spirit has a ministry also to the world, to bring conviction of sin, the offer of righteousness, and a warning of judgment to come (16:8-11). The world rejected Jesus and still does so today (15:18, 20). Despite the world's continued rejection, however, the Spirit continues to convict, and many in the second generation continue to hear Jesus' voice through the voice of the Spirit.

Above all else, the ever-present and available Spirit makes the presence of Jesus real in our lives, even though we can't see Him or touch Him (16:13-15). The Spirit provides a real sense of the supernatural working in those who enter into relationship with Jesus and yield themselves to the Spirit's guidance and comfort. Indeed, it has been better for us that Jesus went away.

CHAPTER 12

Jesus Lays Down His Life for His Friends

John 18:1–19:42

In the Gospel of John, the story of Jesus' crucifixion begins and ends in a garden (18:1; 19:41). It falls naturally into three parts: First, there is a section describing the betrayal, arrest, and indictment of Jesus (18:1-27). The central section is concerned with the trial before Pilate (18:29–19:16). The last part describes the crucifixion and burial of Jesus (19:16-42).

The Last Walk

With a heavy heart John followed Jesus down the stairs leading from the upper room. Jesus had just celebrated the Passover with His disciples—well, with most of His disciples anyway. John had seen Judas leave the room hours ago and knew that, for some reason, he had not returned. Jesus had dropped some dark hints of betrayal in the disciples' ears and left the impression that Judas was the one He was talking about. But that was impossible! There were a number of half-wits among the twelve, but Judas had always been the steady and sensible one! Did Jesus really know something or was He just being suspicious? It did seem strange, though, that Judas hadn't returned. Where had he gone?

As John puzzled over these things, he noticed that Jesus was leading the group to the long, public staircase that worked its way down from Mount Zion toward the Ophel Ridge, just south of the temple. For a while John concentrated on the placement of his feet, working his way downward one step at a time. "Not the greatest piece of work," he grumbled to himself as he noticed anew the unevenness of the steps.

Night had fallen but it was still early. The stair-step street was largely dark, but the occasional house torch supplemented the light of the torches Peter and Nathanael had thought to bring along. John pulled his cloak tighter around him as he felt the chill air of a March evening at Jerusalem's elevation. Gaps between the buildings to the left occasionally allowed glimpses of the brightly lit temple, which looked ever larger and more imposing as they worked their way eastward down the hill. When buildings blocked the view of the temple, they became silhouetted shadows against the yellow glow of the night sky over the temple. Somehow John found himself disinterested in the festivities that would take place there the next day.

Soon they reached the bottom of Mount Zion and climbed the small rise to the top of Ophel Ridge. To the left was the giant marble staircase that Jesus and the disciples had ascended many times to enter the temple courtyard. Tonight, however, Jesus showed no interest in the temple; He was heading elsewhere. Soon they went out the Water Gate and down the steep, winding path from the Ophel Ridge to the Kidron Valley.

They headed north up the valley until the temple was once more above them and to their left. In front of them and to the right was the Mount of Olives, glowing duskily in the spillover of light from the temple mount. Walking around Jerusalem was a great way to stay in shape! Somehow John's legs seemed more tired than usual.

It appeared that Jesus was planning to spend some prayer time in the Garden of Gethsemane again. John wondered what was on His mind this time. What had He meant when He said He was about to leave them? Did it really have something to do with betrayal and death, as He had suggested so often? John's thoughts were turning as dark as the Valley of Kidron in mid-evening.

When they arrived at the Garden, Jesus left eight of the disciples at the entrance as if to guard the place. He took John, Peter, and James into the Garden and left them together while He went on a bit farther to pray. John discovered that more than his legs were tired. He tried praying, but his mind wandered almost immediately. *Let me get comfortable on this patch of grass,* he thought. *I'll just rest my eyes for a couple minutes and then I'll be able to concentrate better on God.*

A sound jolted John awake. He realized with a start that he had been deeply asleep for some time. For a minute he had no idea where he was. As his mind slowly came back to reality, he thought, *That's Judas's voice. He's finally found us. Great! The team is back together again.*

Arrest and Trial Before Annas

John 18:1-27 portrays three major events: Jesus' arrest in the Garden; His interrogation before Annas, the father-in-law of Caiaphas, the high priest; and Peter's three denials of Jesus. In describing the latter two events, John jumps back and forth between the courtyard where Peter is and the interrogation chamber where Jesus is.

The main point of John 18:1-11 seems to be that Jesus is in full control of the situation, in fulfillment of what He had said earlier: "No one takes [my life] from me, but I lay it down of my own accord" (John 10:18). Although Jesus is about to be murdered, John does not portray Him as a victim; He is in control of events. For example, if Jesus had wanted to avoid arrest, He could have simply gone somewhere other than the Garden where Judas knew He often went. But Jesus led His disciples to the Garden even though He knew what would happen there. John describes no anguish in the Garden: Jesus is in full control of His emotions as well. And He doesn't wait for the mob to come to Him, He moves forward and addresses them and shows that He can intimidate them. His death is voluntary. They could not have arrested Him had He not allowed it.

Under the circumstances, Peter's reaction is almost amusing. Although Jesus is fully in control of the situation, Peter sees things as totally out of control and whips out his sword. But Jesus tells him to put the sword away. His good intentions would prevent events from unfolding the way God planned. Jesus must go to the cross or God's plan of salvation would fail. Peter's attempt to gain control of the situation would only have moved things truly out of control.

From the Garden, the scene shifts to Jesus' encounter with Annas. Here, Jesus is quite assertive (18:20-23). He challenges both the secretiveness of His arrest ("I said nothing in secret") and the legal procedures being followed ("Why question me?"). He even tosses in a dash of humor ("If I spoke the truth, why did you strike me?"). Jesus here certainly does not follow an extreme interpretation of His own statement about turning the other cheek (Matt. 5:39)! He protests His opponent's abuse of authority. Evidently, being like Jesus does not mean being a doormat. It is appropriate for Christians to set boundaries in their relationships with others. Allowing other people to walk all over us generally helps no one. There's a definite difference between being humble and being abused.

Only the Gospel of John tells us that more than one disciple followed Jesus into the high priest's courtyard. Presumably, the girl at the door knew that John (the "other disciple") was a disciple of Jesus but didn't challenge him because he had privileged access. Peter was not so lucky. Peter had come boldly to the front at the time of Jesus' arrest. Now that boldness challenges him to further boldness, but he fails the test. Poor, impulsive Peter. Too bold one minute; too timid the next!

Trial Before Pilate

Pilate is the central figure of the next part of the narrative (John 18:28–19:16). Historically, he was in a position of considerable political weakness. A series of blunders had repeatedly offended the religious sensibilities of the Jews. He was, therefore, unpopular with them, and his fitness to rule had even come under suspicion in the palace of the emperor in Rome. One more major conflict with the religious leaders and he would be out of office. This made him extremely vulnerable to blackmail.

In approaching Pilate, the priests formulated their charge against Jesus in the political terms that a Roman governor could appreciate. Jesus must be executed because His kingship was a threat to Caesar. But Jesus' statement "My kingdom is not of this world" made it clear to Pilate that Jesus' claim to kingship was no political or military threat to Rome. Determined to free Jesus but at the same time to provide the Jewish leaders a face-saving way out, he offered to release Jesus on the basis of a traditional prisoner release rather than on a judgment of innocence.

Things got complicated for Pilate when the Jewish leaders rejected his offer. They wanted Jesus dead at any cost. That meant that Pilate must either persuade them against their set opinion or release Jesus in the face of their wrath, which he couldn't afford to do politically. So he was forced into a dilemma between justice and self-interest.

Pilate sought, therefore, to excite the religious leaders' sympathy by flogging Jesus and presenting Him before them. But they refused to be moved. Sensing that Pilate's self-interest had weakened him, the religious leaders started playing dirty; they argued that Jesus should die because He had broken their religious law. Pilate couldn't afford to be seen as allowing sacrilege against the Jewish religion.

Pilate then realized that his indecision was his weakness. He couldn't save both himself and Jesus. He determined to save himself and then some. He'd consent to the religious leaders' request, but they would pay dearly for it. He would condemn Jesus in exchange for their public confession of their obligation to serve Caesar: "We have no king but Caesar."

Earlier, Caiaphas had insisted that one man had to be sacrificed to save the nation (11:48-52). Now he was ready to sacrifice the nation in order to destroy that one man. The religious leaders rejected Jesus' kingship with such passion that they now rejoiced in a king whom they had always hated. Pilate intended to hold them to that pledge in the future. They would have no more power over him. From this point on in the Gospel story, Pilate is unmovable. The death of Jesus made him strong.

The Crucifixion Itself

Crucifixion was a peculiarly Roman form of execution. Some people were nailed to the cross; others were tied with ropes. The key element, however, was that in order to breathe, victims had to push with their feet to raise their bodies somewhat. Death came by suffocation when they became too weary to raise themselves anymore. Death was, therefore, slow and painful. Breaking the legs, of course, would hasten the process, when that was for the executioners' convenience. An additional element of torture was shame and exposure—being hung naked in front of family and friends.

The "new" Pilate struck again at the Crucifixion. The wording he chose for the inscription placed on the cross made Jesus' crucifixion symbolic of Rome's dominance over Palestine and Judaism. With the inscription, he turned the crucifixion into a public spectacle designed as a blow to the prestige of the Jews and their religious leaders. Although Pilate now felt in control of matters, there are repeated reminders in this part of the text that everything is happening according to the predictions placed in the Scriptures (John 19:24, 28, 36, 37). God retains control even when human beings feel they are in control. Jesus' death is voluntary, purposeful, and according to the Scriptures.

What's the Big Deal About the Cross?

When Jesus pronounced the words "It is finished" on the cross (19:30), what exactly was finished? What makes the Cross so special that Paul would refuse to glory in anything else (Gal. 6:14)?

The particular emphasis in the Gospel of John seems to be that the Cross is the fulfillment of the Bible prophecies pointing toward the Messiah. Prophecy was fulfilled right down to the minutest detail of just what type of garment was divided, what type was wagered for (19:23, 24), and just how the body of Jesus was handled after His death (vs. 35-37). The Cross makes it clear that even when bad things happen in our lives, God has foreseen it all ahead of time and is in full control of the situation. We don't need to be afraid.

The law of God was also fulfilled on the Cross. God was never more faithful to His covenant than He was when He dealt the wages of sin (Rom. 6:23) to Jesus as the Representative of the sinful human race. If the law of God could have been changed, humanity could have been saved without the Cross. But the Cross was necessary to the saving of the human race while at the same time preserving the peace and the order of the universe (2 Cor. 5:14, 15). The Cross condemns human sin in the person of Christ (Rom. 8:3; 1 Pet. 2:24), and the Resurrection affirms the whole human race on account of the perfect life of Jesus (Acts 13:32, 33; 2 Cor. 5:21).

Above all else, the Cross affirms the value of the human person. God so loves every human being that Jesus would have died for even one. As a full-fledged member of the Godhead and as the Creator of the universe, Jesus possesses in His person infinite value. In dying for you and me, He testified to the infinite value He places on each of us. You and I are worth everything to Him. And the value that we have in the Cross is a value that does not change no matter what we do or whom we become. We may be the poorest of the poor, yet our value is infinite in the Cross. We may fail a hundred times, yet our value is infinite in the Cross. We may be despised and rejected by everyone we meet, yet our value is infinite in the Cross. And that value is set for eternity. If we should, in the end, choose to reject the Cross, our value in eternity will be measured by the pain God feels at our absence.

When we gain a sense of our value in the Cross, we can begin to avoid the ups and downs that come when our self-worth is based on performance or on the fickle opinions of others. When we see ourselves in the light of the Cross, we develop the strength to overcome sin, the confidence to defeat Satan, and the joy that comes from knowing who we are. No wonder Paul said, "May I never boast except in the cross of our Lord Jesus Christ."

CHAPTER 13

The Power of the Resurrection

John 20:1–21:25

"I still can't believe it," Thomas moaned to his wife in the motel room. "This should never have happened."

"Why didn't you *do* something instead of running away?"

"Did you have to bring that up again? It's embarrassing enough for everyone to know that I spent three years of my life following Someone who turned out to be a fraud. And I just couldn't bear watching Him be crucified," Thomas said for perhaps the twentieth time.

"But He *needed* you," his wife shot back. "I saw Him looking around in that crowd for a friendly face—for someone, anyone, who cared. Were you there? No. Was anyone of the twelve there? No."

"There you go exaggerating again. You yourself said that John went right through the soldiers to the foot of Jesus' cross." Thomas's sorrow was turning to anger for about the twelfth time.

"Oh yes, John did come up to the foot of the cross for a couple minutes, but that was only because Jesus' mother made him take her there. You could see on his face that he really wanted to be someplace else—anyplace else."

"So, what did you do, brave woman?"

"I tried to press as close as I could without getting in the way of the soldiers," she retorted. "But Jesus hardly knew me; what could I have said that would have helped Him, anyway? I've never been a great talker."

"You're gabbing just fine right now. Your mouth always seems to work fine when you're beating *me* up with your words! Out of my way! I've got to get outside for some fresh air."

"Running away again?" She was on a roll now as she followed him partway out the door. "You'd think Jesus gave running lessons, the way you guys behave."

Thomas put his hands over his ears and strode away from the motel and his female "conscience." It was a sunny Monday afternoon, just three days after Jesus had died and been buried. Rumors abounded about strange happenings at His tomb yesterday, but Thomas wouldn't listen to any of it. In his saner moments he was toying with returning to Galilee and looking for a job in the fishing industry. People always had to eat.

He hadn't gone a hundred yards when he saw John coming—goody two-shoes John. He looked really revved up this time. He'd been impossible to live with since Friday. He'd been the closest one to Jesus at the Last Supper on Thursday. The only one at the cross. The first one at the tomb. The one Jesus said He loved the most. You'd think Jesus' death was a blessing, the way John talked. He was the last person Thomas wanted to see just then, but what's the use in being rude when you're running out of friends and even your wife despises you?

"Thomas! I'm so glad I found you here. You're not going to believe this: We saw Him! We saw Him last night. He came right into the room where we had that last supper with Him. He said, 'Peace be with you.' I had my doubts at first, but then He showed us the nail marks in His hands and the wound in His side. It was Him! He's alive!"

John was out of control as usual. Thomas's expression barely changed. Nothing surprised him any more.

"Get a grip on yourself, John," Thomas said evenly. "You've been telling stories all weekend. I really don't have time for this."

"But this is real," John replied earnestly, trying to tone down his enthusiasm for Thomas's sake. "I saw Him. I heard Him. He even ate something in front of us."

"But did you *touch* Him?" Thomas retorted.

"Why would I do that? You just don't go putting your hands all over the Master!"

"Listen to me, John. Unless I see the nail marks in His hands with my own eyes and put my finger where the nails were and put my hand into His side, I will not believe it."

Doubting Thomas

The story about "doubting Thomas" in John 20 is unique among the four Gospels. As we saw at the beginning of this book, John told the story to highlight the contrast between two generations. The first generation knew Jesus in the flesh or knew someone who had known Him. Those in that first generation could base their faith on seeing, hearing, and touching Jesus. The second generation had no such firsthand experience. Of necessity, their faith was based on the written testimonies about Jesus the first generation had put together. They'd never seen Jesus, heard Him, touched Him, or witnessed a spectacular miracle directly from His hand.

At first glance the second generation would seem to be at a great disadvantage. But John uses his Gospel to point out a great advantage for the second generation. Because they hadn't seen or touched Jesus, their faith wasn't dependent on such experiences. It wasn't subject to the ups and downs of daily events. They were less likely to miss the spiritual significance of Jesus' miracles.

In this story, Thomas represents the first generation (see 20:29-31). In order to believe, he needed to touch. He needed miracles to keep up his faith. Consequently, he would miss the blessing Jesus pronounced on second-generation faith (20:29). He would have a much harder time grasping the message of John's gospel—that Jesus' word is as good as His touch, that having the Holy Spirit is even better than having Jesus' physical presence (16:7), that after Jesus left, the disciples would do even greater things than He'd done (14:12). Nevertheless, this story also exhibits God's mercy; in spite of Thomas's struggle to believe, Jesus didn't abandon him; rather, He gave him what he needed (20:24-28).

The Power of His Resurrection

The resurrection of Jesus was the most awesome event of all time. Despite all our wonderful science and technology, we still have no clue how to bring the dead back to life. Anyone who has the power to raise the dead has the power to accomplish anything else that the human race might need. That's why the heart of Christian faith is the testimony that Jesus rose from the dead. The power of the Resurrection has been the basis for the mighty acts of God in the lives of Christians ever since (2 Cor. 5:14-17). The power of the Resurrection is the basis for limitless power in the lives of Christians today.

Why, then, are these "limitless powers" so invisible in many churches? Why is it so hard to see the mighty hand of God in a secular world? *It is simply because we so often forget.* Whenever the Israelites forgot the mighty things that God had done for them, they lost the power of the faith and the sense of His living presence. When they remembered what He had done for them in the past, the power of those past deeds was reactivated in their lives. In fact, the very essence of Old Testament spiritual life was recounting the mighty acts of God in their history. (See for example Deut. 6:20-24; 26:1-12; Psalms 66:1-6; 78:1-55; 105–107.)

Second Chronicles 20 tells of a time when a coalition of three nations threatened the Israelites. Things looked very dark indeed. Then King Jehoshaphat called the people together to pray. If I'd been king, I'd have been begging and pleading (read "whining") for God to do something fast! Instead, Jehoshaphat recited what God had done for Israel in the past (2 Chron. 20:5-12). When he did so, God's mighty power was unleashed. In delicious irony, God caused three armies to be destroyed even though confronted only by a choir (2 Chron. 20:13-25)! When Jehoshaphat reminded God how He'd delivered Israel during the Exodus, the power of the Exodus was unleashed once more.

What was true in Old Testament times is also true of New Testament times. The mightiest act of God is what He did at the Cross and at Jesus' resurrection. And the secret of Christian power is the constant retelling of the Christ event. Talking about Jesus is no empty retelling. The power of the Resurrection is unleashed in the life of all those who tell others about what Christ has done for them.

That's why sharing our faith is such an essential part of Christian experience. Where there is no retelling of the mighty acts of God, there is no power. But telling what God has done brings revival and reformation to the church. The power of the Resurrection turns a formal religion into a living and powerful one!

Today's generation has little interest in a cold, formal, legalistic religion. Why should they? It's boring and lifeless. It saps the energy and burdens the spirit. The antidote is to become part of the living and active power of God by remembering and retelling what God has done: what God did in Old Testament times, what God did at the Cross, and what God has done and is doing in our own experience. Real Christianity is never boring and lifeless. Real Christianity is filled with awesome power and excitement. It makes no sense to settle for less.

The Epilogue to the Gospel

John 21 comprises the epilogue to the Gospel. The centerpiece of this epilogue is a fishing story in which Jesus demonstrates once more His ability to act from a distance to provide what disciples need. He provides breakfast for them. In that context comes a brief but fascinating conversation with Peter. In this conversation, Jesus demonstrates His willingness to accept His followers, even when their discipleship falls short of God's ideal.

Jesus questions Peter three times about the depth of their relationship, no doubt in intentional response to Peter's three denials of Jesus described in John 18:15-18, 25-27. The first time, Jesus says, "Do you love me *more than these [the other disciples]?*" Jesus needed to draw Peter out on this point because he had been so quick earlier to boast that his loyalty exceeded that of the others (Matt. 26:33). When Peter refuses to respond to that part of the question, Jesus accepts his silence as confession and does not press the point further. What counts is the depth of your relationship with Jesus, not how well your relationship compares with that of others.

Verses 15-17 describe a threefold repetition of question, reply, and response. This is unexpected and could even seem rude on the part of Jesus. The effect is to probe Peter to the depths of his being, at the cost of considerable pain. Peter's self-confidence and assertiveness are gradually chipped away, until he is left with nothing but the certainty that Jesus knows his heart and will be fair in His judgments.

"No pain, no gain" seems to be a law of spiritual growth. Those who have advanced far in spiritual life are usually those who have suffered much. There is something about pain, loss, poverty, and emotional anguish that can bring people to the place where they can make major gains in spiritual development. And sometimes, as happened in the case of Peter, the author of that pain is Jesus Himself, who, like a loving surgeon, wounds so that He might heal. Jesus doesn't settle for quick, superficial answers. He insists on getting down to the true feelings and motives of those He loves. The process, however, usually demands a price.

In the text, the threefold dialogue seems to take place in the presence of the other disciples at the breakfast location. But verse 20 implies that Jesus and Peter are walking alone along the beach. Ellen White suggests that after Peter's response to the third question, he and Jesus headed down the beach, and the rest of their conversation occurred as they walked along.[1] If so, the exchange recorded in verses 15-17 happened in front of the other disciples. So, Peter's confession was not for his sake alone. The other disciples needed to regain confidence in Peter after his terrible betrayal of Jesus in the high priest's courtyard. Public sin needs to be publicly confessed in order for one to get a truly fresh start in life.

What to Do When You've Stumbled Spiritually

As was the case with Peter, your relationship with Jesus will tend to have ups and downs. You'll know times of tremendous joy and spiritual strength. Then you'll stumble into an old sin and, like Peter, start questioning whether Jesus could possibly accept you any more. Satan will keep throwing that sin in your face, trying to shatter your confidence in Christ.

What would Jesus have us do when we fall? What is the path to a full restoration of the joy of relationship with Jesus?

1. Know what God is like. What is God like? " 'I know the plans I have for you,' declares the Lord, 'plans to prosper you and not to harm you, plans to give you hope and a future' " (Jer. 29:11). God is not like us, sitting around thinking the worst about others. God's plans are plans to prosper us, not to destroy us. God is on our side.

We see this God in the book of Jeremiah, planning seventy years ahead of time to deliver His unfaithful people and restore them to their land. We see this God in His incredible forgiveness of David, one of the great sinners of all time. We see Him in the father who welcomed back the prodigal son. We see a God who welcomes sinners from Nicodemus to the Samaritan woman, from the most faithful of church members to the most jaded of criminals, be they Jew or Gentile, rich or poor, male or female.

When we've fallen back into sin we must remind ourselves that God loves sinners. God forgives sinners. God accepts sinners— sometimes, even before they ask. God gives sinners new life. The message here is not that sin doesn't matter. It's that no matter what you've done, you can start over today. Note the incredible text in 1 Timothy 1:15, 16:

> Here is a trustworthy saying that deserves full acceptance: Christ Jesus came into the world to save sinners—of whom I am the worst. But *for that very reason* I was shown mercy so that in me, the worst of sinners, Christ Jesus might

display his unlimited patience as an example for those who would believe on him and receive eternal life (emphasis supplied).

You think you've been bad? Paul claimed that he was the ultimate sinner, the absolute worst. Did that remove His access to the grace and mercy of God? To the contrary! It was *"for that very reason"* that he received mercy from Jesus. Our Lord picked him out as an example to show us how deep His mercy goes. It is at those very times when you feel the worst that you have the greatest claim on His mercy! The more you need Him, the more ready He is to make an example of you through His unlimited patience and mercy. *That's* the kind of God you are dealing with!

2. Tell the truth about yourself. The Bible calls this confession. Confession is simply facing reality and being honest with God about it. Confession is about taking responsibility for your actions. There may have been mitigating circumstances. You may have stumbled into it. But confession doesn't make excuses; it just looks the truth in the eye and says, "I blew it! I chose to be inattentive. I chose to sin because it looked like fun. I chose to put myself in a place where accidents can happen. I lost focus in my relationship to You."

Confession is about exposing darkness to the light.

Everyone who does evil hates the light, and will not come into the light for fear that his deeds will be exposed. But whoever lives by the truth comes into the light, so that it may be seen plainly that what he has done has been done through God (John 3:20, 21).

Exposing our darkness to the light can be very painful. Our sense of self-worth will rebel against the shock. But if we are grounded in the value that we have at the Cross, if we are conscious of the kind of God we are dealing with, we can move ahead with our confession, because not moving ahead leaves us in the midst of Peter's agony of remorse, guilt, and lost relationship. Anything but that!

3. Ask for forgiveness. It's that simple. You needn't suffer weeks and weeks of penance to show God just how sorry you really are. "If we confess our sins, he is faithful and just and will forgive us our sins and purify us from all unrighteousness" (1 John 1:9). God doesn't keep throwing our mistakes in our face; it's Satan who does that. God doesn't stack up a bunch of conditions before He is willing to forgive. Those conditions were already met in Jesus Christ. "No matter how many promises God has made, they are 'Yes' in Christ" (2 Cor. 1:20).

I know from personal experience that forgiving can be one of the toughest things we do, whether it's forgiving others or forgiving ourselves. I remember a boss who did some things that hurt me. I knew that I should forgive him. I wanted to forgive him. I told myself over and over that I was forgiving him. And yet my stomach churned whenever he was around. It took years for me to get over it and truly feel free in his presence.

The good news is that God is not like that! In sending Jesus, He demonstrated that His heart has already changed toward us! There is absolutely no reason for us to fear Him. His stomach is not churning in our presence. He loves us and is willing to forgive. All we have to do is be willing to be forgiven. Is that really so hard? Yes, it can be, but as we allow the truths of John's Gospel to permeate our hearts, we gradually gain the confidence to confess our sins and ask for the forgiveness He has already provided. What a gracious God!

4. Plan to forsake that sin forever. Paul wrote, "Clothe your-selves with the Lord Jesus Christ, and do not think about how to gratify the desires of the sinful nature" (Rom. 13:14). How can you do this when sin may even be fun at times? There are two things you should do. First, write down the consequences of con-tinuing in sin. The consequences of sexual sin, for example, in-clude spiritual indecisiveness, secretiveness, the loss of a sense of Jesus' approval and presence, guilt and shame that destroy your sense of self-worth, regrets, and difficulties in your marriage both now and later on. Read the list every time you are tempted, and ask yourself whether a few moments of pleasure are worth all that. Doing this can go a long way toward making that sin distasteful to you.

Second, rearrange your life to minimize the chance of a further relapse. If you want to stop drinking, don't go to the parts of town where the bars are, avoid stores that sell alcohol, and spend as little time as possible with "friends" who like to drink socially. If you're struggling sexually, get rid of all the suggestive material in your house, arrange your life to avoid the flirt in the office, and ask a trusted friend to hold you accountable in thought and deed.

There is absolutely nothing that can compare with the feeling that comes from being at peace with God, from being totally com-mitted to His will. There is nothing like the joy that comes when your conscience is clean and nothing stands between you and God or between you and anybody else.

You can go through the motions and call the experience Chris-tianity, but why settle for less than the real thing? There's nothing like it. You'll find it in the beloved Gospel.

---

1. See *The Desire of Ages*, 815.